Internet Marketing Manifesto

Everything you wanted to know about marketing on the world's #1 platform.

PETE GARCIA

STARDOM BOOKS

STARDOM BOOKS

WORLDWIDE

www.StardomBooks.com

STARDOM BOOKS

A Division of Stardom Publishing

and infoYOGIS Technologies.

105-501 Silverside Road

Wilmington, DE 19809

FIRST EDITION AUGUST 2019

Stardom Books

Internet Marketing Manifesto/ Everything you wanted to know about marketing on the world's #1 platform.

PETE GARCIA

p. 144
cm. 13.5 X 21.5

Category: Marketing/Internet

ISBN-13: 978-1-7332116-3-5

ISBN-10: 1-7332116-3-2

DEDICATION

This book is dedicated to all of you who have braved the struggles and looking at progressing in the digital world. The Internet started off as a defense project, but with its growth during the last two decades, it's now ubiquitous. Marketing on this all-pervasive platform brings about its own opportunities and challenges, and this book is dedicated to all the marketers who have tested the new medium and shared their wisdom.

CONTENTS

ACKNOWLEDGMENTS

You have seen them often. You pick up a book and get to this section, and find that the author, once again, has dedicated the book to someone else and not you. Some unknown, non-existent assistant or some casual reference to famous people.

Not this time.

I would like to thank YOU for taking the time to get this book. I would be even more grateful if you read the book and take ACTION to further your life and create a positive difference.

78%
65%
72%
98%
WWW.YOURWEBSITE.COM

1
INTRODUCTION TO INTERNET MARKETING

"What internet marketing really, really, truly is all about!"

An Introduction on Internet Marketing

Internet Marketing, put rather simply, is the idea of regular marketing, both to customers and to other companies (B2B), using the power of the Internet.

Nevertheless, entering the idea and looking at how it works may not be thought about as quite so basic. The primary factor for this is that the Internet, still fairly young, is constantly evolving with new technology and innovation.

New advances in Web technology are continuously supplying new chances for businesses to add to their marketing technique and material. Today essentially all income levels can be considered in the Internet Marketing methods of service.

In the 1990s, Internet Marketing went crazy. It was a

brand new concept, and caution had actually been thrown to the wind in all the hype. Companies did not take into consideration that the exact same variables of marketing in other types of media ought to logically be applied to Internet Marketing too. Their failure to study markets and develop sound strategies resulted in the fall of numerous so-called dot-coms in the end of 2000. The survivors, and successors, started to look toward time- evaluated reasoning in marketing for ideas, and the result was huge development in this sector.

Through the now-tweaked method of online marketers and businesses alike, targeted advertising on the Internet has actually brought forth excellent success. Essentially any market you may wish to enter into can be tapped on the Internet. Numerous marketing firms provide the services a business needs to get their offers out to consumers, while a small business may wish to handle their marketing on their own or can find low-cost options for their objectives as well.

Search engines are a significant resource for marketing, but typically are just able to provide results for what the customer is currently looking for. To achieve the spontaneous recommendations provided by tv or radio, pop-up ads and ads positioned directly on a web-site are used. Email is an outstanding type of marketing, but generally just has success once a company has actually developed a great relationship with the consumer.

A growing number of people are investing plenty of time on the Internet daily.

The idea is simple: the convenience provided by the Internet, coupled with the increasing abilities of the Internet to assist you get your jobs finished, has actually allowed for all types of services to be conducted with point and click ease. Many tasks no longer need a trip in the car to be completed.

Hence, relationships are growing online, and as they do, the speed of Internet commerce has actually soared into the trillions of dollars. Advances in innovation, and increased traffic, are causing a future for Internet Marketing that can only point skyward.

What Internet Marketing Is?

Internet Marketing is the business of both marketing and offering items and services online. This kind of business is ever-increasing in popularity, with millions of individuals now making purchases on the Internet.

Internet Marketing started in the early 1990s as mainly a way of item description, consisting simply of text descriptions. As innovation progressed, Internet Marketing quickly advanced to include pictures and other rich graphics as part of ads for products and services. After understanding the remarkable capacity of this methods of marketing, Internet-based companies started opening their virtual doors for business.

As opposed to what are now referred to as "brick and mortar" operations, these e-businesses offer their services and products to a growing variety of customers, conducting all, or nearly all, of their service in the virtual world of the Internet.

There are lots of types of marketing on the Internet. Amongst them are short article marketing, blog marketing, e-mail marketing, online search engine marketing (to include search engine optimization), banner advertisements, pay-per-click advertisements, and pop-up ads.

It is very important to note that each of these kinds catches the attention of the target audience in various ways, and some might be more reliable than others depending on the product and services, the target audience, and the technique and goal of the business marketing itself.

Amongst the business functions that might require use of various methods in their strategies are customer service, sales, public relations, information management, and others.

Internet Marketing has likewise end up being an essential component of many "traditional" operations, however online-only companies have actually offered some challenge in the arena of retail sales, an example of business-to-consumer (B2C) marketing, business-to-business (B2B) marketing, and peer-to-peer (P2P) marketing. However, other online-only businesses have actually specialized into newer techniques, such as online auctions, websites that allow you to find the very best price on what you're looking for, and likewise websites that allow you to name your own cost.

Even more, affiliate online marketers have actually emerged, offering marketing services to virtually all types of service. These companies typically get what is called pay for performance. Even home-based businesses now thrive thanks to Internet Marketing.

There are lots of benefits to the principle of Internet Marketing. It enables customers to conduct and shop service from the convenience of their own home, any time of day or night, or from essentially anywhere supplied they have connection to the Internet. Services work far more effectively with partners.

Efficiency and speed have actually increased significantly as business and shopping have actually relocated to the Internet. Even expenses have been drastically decreased. Moreover, at this time, it is uncommon that you need to pay any tax for the items you acquire online.

The most noted downsides to Internet Marketing are the

unreliable or sometimes slow Web connections that take place, and online security. Innovation is diligently pursuing solutions to both issues, and development is being made. Also, with the attention of the federal government on identity theft, it is clear that security and dependability will continue to improve gradually.

What Internet Marketing is Not

As with all things new, it is very easy for us to end up being involved the development, the convenience, and the excitement we experience with something never ever offered to us previously. Internet Marketing is no exception. Despite the apparent benefits provided by this new medium for commerce and company in general, Internet Marketing does have its restrictions. It is also easy for us to presume that a new item or technology can do more than it really can.

Following are some consider considering what Internet Marketing is not.

Initially to consider is that Internet Marketing is NOT a replacement for the standard ways of shopping and/or selling. Assume for a moment that you are looking to purchase a diamond ring for someone unique. You go online, browse through picture after photo, discover some eligible and really beautiful pieces, which's where you stop. You can't feel that ring, nor can you take a close look at the diamond. You have only a minimal scope of what the merchandise will be like when you physically possess it. Are you going to pay potentially countless dollars for that ring, or will you go to a local jeweler rather, where you can get a far better idea of what you're buying? This is a key limitation to Internet Marketing for lots of products.

Internet Marketing is likewise NOT a fail-proof system.

Nearly everyone who conducts any form of business or shopping online has experienced the temporary unavailability of a website. The site goes down, and you can't get your business done when you had planned.

When you compare the number, who have had such wild success, with all the businesses who have failed or never really taken off online, you will find that the "overnight" millionaires are not the standard of what Internet Marketing is. Success in Internet Marketing requires a lot of hard work, just as any other type of business venture requires.

Internet Marketing, finally, is NOT today what it will be tomorrow. As fast as one design of computer system replaces another, so do the alternatives provided in the world of Internet Marketing Just fifteen years ago you could go online and discover bit more than text-based item descriptions. Now look at what you can find on the Internet. Whole stores exist online, and their number is growing. In addition, laws on everything from individual security to taxation are altering and guarantee to make a various landscape of Internet Marketing than the one we see today.

The Pros of Internet Marketing

Internet Marketing began its presence with some integrated benefits. With the development of faster speeds and much better web-site graphics, to name a few factors, the benefits have actually continued to grow at a remarkable speed. Businesses and consumers alike have had a virtually insatiable need for more, better, and faster access to products and service throughout the spectrum of Internet Marketing.

There is no indication of a change in this trend, therefore the number of Internet consumers, along with the number of benefits, for Internet Marketing will continue to grow.

Without a doubt, one of the greatest benefits offered by Internet Marketing is the convenience it furnishes. At any time of day or night, any day of the year, you can go online and shop or conduct your service. And you can do this from anywhere you want, provided the place has a computer system with Web access.

And now, if you have a laptop with cordless connection, you really are endless in your option of locations to connect.

For the marketer, the Internet offers fast and cheap solutions to many of the problems of advertising. It is cheaper for your company to blast out a million e-mail advertisements to your customer list than it would be for you to do the same by traditional postal mail.

Expect your company operates without Internet Marketing, and it simply discovered that a particular item your company markets is being phased out by your supplier to make way for an updated design. You choose to run a sale to clear your stock, but you've just sent out your sales advertisement, and now it'll be a couple days before the update can reach your consumers. Just those who come to your outlets will understand sooner. However, your competitor, with the same situation, markets on the Internet. That rival will beat you to the punch by zapping a fast e-mail to all of its clients, who will see the sale far faster. This benefit cannot easily be disregarded.

Lastly, Internet Marketing provides unparalleled access to a broader consumer base than you can discover anywhere else worldwide. Think about a business like the one you have, or hope to begin, without Internet Marketing. The best you can wish for from that one establishment is access to the city you lie in which city's next-door neighbors. Without developing more outlets, you will not get a bigger consumer base. However, with Internet Marketing, you have access to anybody who goes to, throughout the world. With the variety of Internet users constantly growing, your consumer base is growing, and it will one day reach into the billions.

The Cons of Internet Marketing.

That being said, there are definitely some disadvantages to Internet Marketing. As you read, bear in mind that much of what Internet Marketing involves consists of ever-changing practices an approach, and therefore much of what is now considered a disadvantage may disappear, and sometimes new disadvantages may arise.

One of the important things most customers value when shopping is human interaction. When a client goes to the shop, she or he can receive direction, recommendations, information, and service from a live individual. The Internet has no such advantage, and lots of consumers shy away from the impersonal nature of Internet shopping.

While live chat and telephone service are frequently offered, Internet Marketing still has a long way to go to overcome this hurdle. So, while a consumer may go to the Web for item information, they may eventually pick to purchase the product personally anyway.

Another important thing to remember is that Internet Marketing is not a totally free activity. The expenses of Internet Marketing consist of such things as web-site design, the online distribution costs of software, advertising and hardware, maintenance, and others. However, some might argue that the physical company brings expenses that Internet Marketing does not. Expenses are pointed out here because, depending on who reads, the expenses still might be deemed a disadvantage.

While your site is open for company 24/7, there are some

problems, both on your end and on the customer's. He or she may very well decide to make their purchase in the store instead if the consumer is having trouble accessing the Internet for some reason. And if your website goes down, you cannot make sales.

Furthermore, if this occurs frequently, clients will quickly despair in the reliability of your site.

Security has led numerous customers to avoid the Web for shopping. Many individuals have a worry of identity theft and other types of scams that keep them from performing their organisation online. While you may have gone to excellent lengths to guarantee your site is, some customers will not be convinced, and won't even offer fundamental info for the purpose of your e-mail marketing.

A significant percentage of the population still does not have access to the Internet, and therefore can never get to your site. What's more, if all of your marketing is conducted online, you and the unconnected consumer are in two different worlds and may never meet.

Much like a snowboarding shop in Miami, you may find yourself with a fantastic product and no direct exposure to the ideal consumers.

How to Win the Internet Marketing War

Ultimately, in any company, you are a rival. The point of competition is to win. Nobody enters into organisation saying "I wish to begin a company that will struggle to endure." Winning is what it's everything about, and in the Internet Marketing war, you're going to need to be devoted to success and keen on your market if you prepare to stand an opportunity. It's no mishap that this is called the Internet Marketing "war". Competitors is fiercer no place than it is on the Internet. And with the huge amount of information out there, you have actually got to rise to the leading just to be seen. Anywhere else, this may sound like putting the cart before the horse, however on the Internet you must have a running start to get market share.

As in an earlier example, you will not do much company offering snowboards in Miami. The skill of effectively targeting the consumers in your market will lead to success. It is very important to bear in mind that, with a lot competitors and choice on the Internet, yours must be the most appealing ad, or you run the risk of being passed over for the first, and last, time. Make certain you understand your market, and your customer, and you might even exceed the fundamentals and spend for marketing research. Simply keep in mind that the expenses can end up being substantial.

One of the most notable means by which to advertise for your site or your product is article writing. The more specific, accurate, and informative your articles, the better are your chances of luring a potential customer to your site.

You might either compose your own, or pay for someone else to compose for you. Simply make sure that grammar and spelling are accurate. Excellent details displayed well will make you look like a specialist in the topic of the post.

E-mail marketing is one of the most direct, and effective, ways to reach your customers. E-mail marketing provides you the opportunity to build a relationship with that customer. As mentioned previously, the impersonal nature of the Internet is a major sticking point for some shoppers.

Much of what you will do to win the Internet Marketing war will truly be up to you. If you base your campaign on full and accurate knowledge, you've got a great weapon on your side in the Internet Marketing war.

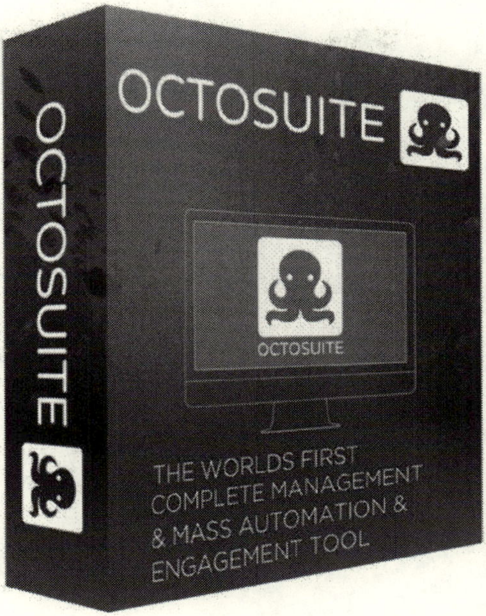

OCTOSUITE
https://bit.ly/2lZWISb

2
LAUNCHING YOUR INTERNET BUSIINESS

"Turn on Your PC and Prepare to Connect To The Internet For Fun and Profits!"

The Significance of Preparation

Not knowing the market, the competitors, and the environment of company were simply a few of the factors that might have been dealt with and avoided with proper preparation. It is essential in today's world of Internet Marketing that preparation is conducted thoroughly. Consider the following as actions in your strategy.

When planning you must be able to note both the advantages and the possible drawbacks of the product or service you are selling. Through planning at this stage you can prevent the prospective problems associated with an item by developing methods to remedy or even compensate for that deficiency.

Choosing what type of project, you will run is very

essential too. What is your budget? What is your staffing need? What will be the time-frame for the marketing project? These and other questions, some of which will depend solely on your special situation, must be asked and answered at this moment of the planning process. With the details laid out in front of you, it will be much easier to see simply what obstacles and constraints you might have to overcome in order to effectively bring and launch out your marketing project. Also, don't forget, this is a business- large effort. Marketing staff should not be the only personnel involved. Interdepartmental communication is important.

Be sure to rely on the most important of all means first: sales and customer feedback. No matter what business you are in, these two factors will exist in one form or another, and they are crucial pieces of data you can use to fine-tune your strategy.

When the project is over, perform an exhaustive review of the whole procedure from beginning to end. Try to find any indications of problem, and likewise for points of excellence, and make note of them for your next campaign. Marketing is a finding out procedure whenever you do it, and just by noting what went right and wrong last time will you know where to position your focus next time.

While this is a really compact overview of the procedure, one typical thread needs to be stitched throughout: Understand, at every step in the process, of the strengths and weak points of the company, of your staff, of the item, and of the marketplace. Just through this awareness can you make a reliable strategy, and just through reliable planning will you be successful in Internet Marketing.

Ways of Making Money Online

Earning money online is not always going to be simple,

and there is certainly no proven way to get rich fast, however your opportunities to get into selling on the Internet are practically endless. Whether you are looking to make a go at it online as a new business, or if you're seeking to broaden the potential customers of your existing service, the Web offers you the opportunity to do practically whatever it is you wish.

For the physical, brick-and-mortar business, taking your offers to the web is going to provide you some spectacular improvements. When you construct your website, you are providing a hassle-free option to your consumers that they will certainly appreciate. When they don't have the time to make it to your location, they can go to your website and do a lot of the same things they would perform in person.

You can also collect e-mail contact information from your customers and visitors and utilize this as a more affordable, quicker means of contacting them and providing essential information.

Organisations existing mostly on the Internet can make money in a variety of methods.

Large or small, these companies can take the type of retail, wholesale, auction, clearing houses, affiliate online marketers, specialized online marketers, banks and other service companies, publishers, blogs (blogs), and countless other types.

Whatever you can potentially imagine a market for, you can make a business online for it. Surprisingly, the Web has even enabled the development of never before seen markets with a voracious consumer appetite.

The individual can also benefit significantly from Internet Marketing. If you're not aiming to start a business, per se, you have many other options. Numerous websites offer you the chance to market your skills as an independent developer, web designer, writer, and lots of other disciplines. Lots of have picked this path, while others have chosen to either market their own products, or to market products with resale rights, on web auction websites. Authors can now release their own books and market them online, maintaining much of the revenue lost otherwise to a publisher. The point is, whatever skill or interest you have, there is probably a market for it on the Internet. And where there is a market, there is an opportunity to make money.

The chances for making money online will depend on many factors, but the most important of those factors is you. While the innovations of the Internet provide new paths to success, the values that achieve success are still the same.

Getting all the Essential Tools You Need

Whereas, with many services, you will require all manner of specialized tools and devices, the number of required tools to start your business online are fairly few. A few of the tools are common to all forms of Internet-based services, and some of them will be dependent on what services or product you use. Those will actually need you to pick your own what is required, and they will not be gone over here because of their specialized nature.

The very first, most obvious thing you will need for an online business is a computer. Be aware that the computer you buy for this business will need to have the capacity to meet the workload you place on it, so a bit of research into the particulars of your market will be helpful. If the computer does not have these, you will need to buy them before going further.

Choose an Internet service provider, necessary to link to the Internet, who offers e-mail. Many ISPs provide e-mail as part of their service. It will be practical to inspect the company's dependability and dependability. Similar to a computer that fails, an ISP that fails you will cost you money and time that you may not be able to afford.

You will also need some additional online tools in order to start your business. This will be unique to your business.

A number of other tools you will need might not have actually struck you as such. Nevertheless, without these tools you will have no chance to get everything going. The very first is money, and it is apparent what cash will provide for your service. The second is time. Time really becomes a tool when you are running a service. Used efficiently, it will serve you well. Used improperly, it will not work for you. The 3rd of these tools is info. Details is the life-blood of the Internet and almost whatever operates around it. Collecting info will take research, time, and often even money.

These are the tools that are important to the conduct of organisation online. Without any among these you will be not able to earn a profit. With them, you are on your method to one of the most exciting opportunities ever.

Choosing Your Web Business Design

Picking your Internet business model is one of those choices you simply can't prevent. If you're preparing to go into business online, you will need to comprehend what you're entering into, and to what degree you wish to be included. Many aspects will play into this choice, and the more believed you take into it, the better your opportunities for a positive outcome will be.

The very best way to pick what organisation model you require is to begin by taking a look at yourself. How much money do you need to purchase this endeavor? Likewise, think of just how much time you are willing and able to dedicate to business. Will you be able to achieve this while still having spare time, and how will this affect your regular task? It is extremely suggested that you do not stop your position with your employer till you've had time to develop your online company and it has shown lucrative enough to change your work earnings.

Once you've worked through the essential self-checks of the business venture, it's time to start taking a look at the models that work. Leave it to the expert veterans to try to fix a broken business model.

If you are planning to sell products or services over the Internet, e-commerce is a model to consider. This might mean retail, wholesale, affiliate programs, and numerous others. If you wish to sell your product, or sell for another person, you could likewise think about the alternative of using an auction site, such as Ebay or Amazon, to conduct your business.

Another option, if you are not wanting to sell a product, is a content-rich site. This is a site where you use informative or entertaining content to audiences, and the cash you get is from advertisements placed on your site. If you feel that this is not going to work for you, you can deal with a similar idea: the subscription site. Here your cash comes directly from the subscriptions spent for by your visitors.

More thorough models exist. If you wish to have a customer base that needs software created particularly for their service, you might need to build your website as an information spot for what you can providing, and consist of some important information on your policies. Another design to consider is an applications design, where you offer access to a particular application for a cost.

You might even be an assistance company, and you can then build around the support services model.

At any rate, you have a lot of alternatives. Which one you pick will depend on what you want to do, and likewise on how much cash and time you can dedicate. Do your research study, look at sites similar to what you plan, and you'll get a great concept of which design to pick.

Why Have Your Own Domain Name?

You're working out your plans to start a new online business. You know that the more you stand out, the more noticeable your business is, the better your chances are for success.

If you are just starting, nobody knows your business yet, so they're going to need some reason to believe it is safe to visit your site. With a domain name chosen by you, you are separating yourself from the clutter of sites that start with something like www.geocities.com/blahblahblah.

Beyond trustworthiness and trustworthiness is a sense of respect and accomplishment. Just as if you had a store in town, and you understood it was essential to the image of the store that you keep it clean, organized and well-kept, a distinct domain provides you that necessary picture of respectability. It likewise states to people who would visit your website that you have actually accomplished something, and that you are not some grassroots start-up that can barely afford the basics.

If you can develop that type of trustworthiness, reliability, regard and achievement that consumers are looking for, you've all at once won over another group of individuals who will be of fantastic importance to you: marketers. If an advertiser knows that people are most likely to visit your site, she or he knows the traffic will be excellent. The marketing dollars will come your method.

Convenience and ease are fantastic advantages to having your own domain. Simply envision for a moment that Amazon.com was not that easy. Rather you needed to remember www.geocities.com/amazon_832576/. For most people such a site address would be impossible to keep in mind.

However, www.amazon.com is remarkably simple to keep in mind therefore traffic improves to that site.

Another essential point about having your own domain name is that you take it with you. If you ever need to leave your existing web host and transfer to another, you get to keep the very same domain name anywhere you go. So if you've put years of effort into your company, and you have to move, possibilities are consumers will not even understand the difference, and your service will continue undisturbed.

The name is associated with the success, and so with your own domain name you can take your success with you.

Protecting Your Own Web Host

Securing your own web host is a very important part of getting your online business going. Without a web host you won't be able to create the website you need to conduct your business. This is business.

The first thing you require to do is consider your company model and your prepare for what it will ultimately become. You need to discover a web host who is reputable if you prepare to have a smoothly run operation. It is really crucial that you inspect around to see what others may be saying about the particular web host you're considering. The last thing you want to do is invest half of your workday combating with an undependable web host. Make certain to check on things like billing, customer support, and any other elements that would indicate to you that this is either a good or a bad location to be.

You need to know what your budget is. Don't worry, there are affordable plans that will meet your needs.

In order to help the representative a little better, a 2nd element you ought to understand is what the needs of your online company will be. Among the essential elements of webhosting requirement are traffic to the site, the variety of e-mail addresses you will require, cgi-bin (for sophisticated site design), and area. If you are uncertain about any of these aspects, the web hosting representative will be able to assist you through.

Once you have actually worked out the information of your requirement, and of the rate of the plan, you're practically done. The only remaining indicate consider and discuss with your representative are additional costs and the web host's area. Find out if you will need PPP access if the host is not local. One specific charge to be knowledgeable about is month-to-month data transfer bandwidth. Know how much you require, and understand what the consequential costs are for going beyond that limit. If whatever checks out, sign up and you're done.

Congratulations, you've simply secured your own web host!

3
SELECTING YOUR NICHE

"Discover a Particular Niche and Lead It!"

Specific Niche Marketing Essentials

Particular niche marketing is an interesting component of the Online marketing world. The word niche has numerous meanings, yet in this context we are discussing an extremely specialized market. Sellers supply a prime example of just what this suggests. A huge chain store supplies literally hundreds of items for sale in the same structure. A mom and pop store will use a much smaller sized number of items, however chances are that these products are of a special brand or are distinct in some other method.

That's precisely just how specific niche marketing functions, on the internet too.

To begin with, specific niche marketing is an excellent choice for the Internet start-up that doesn't have the capability to compete with a bigger seller. Cash needs as well as workload are simply 2 of the many restricting variables to beginning such a major operation. Nonetheless, particular niche marketing needs considerably lower expenses and also a much lighter work. This will certainly be a fantastic benefit to any person beginning an Internet company.

The way it works is quite simple. You do the research on your item, as well as you learn who's wanting that item. Once you know who you're searching for, you figure out where they often tend to congregate in the on-line neighborhood. On-line sites where you can always discover individuals gathered by their passions are places such as forums, subscriber lists, and newsgroups, all of which provide the visitor an opportunity to publish as well as participate. Discovering the consumers you want for your service is as simple as doing a search for the sort of topic you would like to explore online. You participate in the discussions and add in a note regarding your items and also where they can be located at the end of your blog posts.

Make sure you are putting your ad on a site appropriate for your business, and that the ad is highly visible. Make sure also that you are using sites with a good reputation and plenty of traffic.

The fact that particular niche markets are so excellent is because you are not investing all of your time trying to inform countless people about your countless items. You are instead telling an extremely narrowed bunch of individuals that are likely to be interested in your handful of products. You spend less time on marketing, as well as much less time on retailing and also inventory. Instead, you optimize your earnings of a much smaller stock with people that are far more likely to purchase. It's genuinely a win-win situation for the buyer as well as the seller online.

How to Recognize an Existing Demand

Recognizing an existing need for your online service is absolutely important to any type of opportunity for success. Whatever your product and service is, locating the niche market to offer it in is just not nearly enough. You might be fortunate and strike a golden goose, however possibilities are that your shot in the dark will be a bad one. It's much better to put in the time to analyze the demand for a particular service or product prior to you put in all that effort.

This is one of those locations of company where you're most likely to have to do some research to get what you desire. To better serve your purpose, it would be helpful for you to first come up with a list of the different niches you are considering.

As soon as you have the list, make a note on how you plan to do your study. A comparison of the results between the specific niches you research will certainly offer you an idea on which ones will provide the most effective chances for success.

One way you can research the demand for a particular product or service is to join the forums previously mentioned. Look for people making comments about something they're looking for but just can't seem to find.

RSS feed on the Internet can help you in your research study. Through these feeds you can enter search phrases and keywords. The search will give you the number of times in a provided duration that those searches were done. One more method is to consider the variety of clicks. Clicks as well as hits are great methods to learn simply how much need there is for the particular niche you're investigating. The greater the number, generally the higher the demand is for service or products in that specific niche.

You will want to do this when you find a niche where

you've realized that there are very few sites in operation. The reason is that there could only be a few sites because the demand is low in that niche.

If you do your research study, chances are that you will certainly discover a couple of great opportunities, and numerous not-so-great ones too. This is where you can make a great business choice about what specific niche to get in, and stay clear of that dangerous shot in the dark.

Common Mistakes in Researching Your Specific niche

When you prepare to start your research on the specific niches you have actually chosen, make sure you understand these typical errors prior to you proceed. These mistakes can do some serious damage to your outcomes, and possibly to your spending plan, if you end up choosing the incorrect specific niche to go into based upon faulty research.

Keep in mind, these are niches. A web site devoted to cars is not running in a particular niche market. However, if you break it down, you can establish a checklist of the particular niches under the umbrella of cars and trucks. Examples of niche markets could be points such as vintage autos, or a website devoted to a particular model of cars and everything there is to learn about it. The factor is that you intend to be as certain as possible when you investigate a particular niche. If you study based solely on "autos" after that you are going to believe there's a huge market packed with prospective clients available. When you get down to the niche, you'll find instead that there really is no reason to think that thousands of enthusiasts will flock to your site about cars!

You want to spend some real time on this now so you aren't spending that time later wondering what went wrong. What many people fail to do is to look carefully through the

Internet for a number of keywords and search phrases, so the researcher is not actually finding a complete plethora of data to analyze.

This is genuinely a word of caution: DON'T make the mistake of getting obsessive in this step. You would certainly be stunned at just exactly how easy it is to be so passionate about what you're doing that you taint the study data you accumulate. You have to be impartial when you do this study. Sure, it's interesting understanding that you're most likely to open an online organisation. If you let emotions get in the way, chances are you will find yourself looking over the research you collected wondering just where you went wrong and why your business is failing.

Just because you think dogwood- scented candles smell great, and you found only one site offering them for sale, and that site claims the candles to be a best-seller, does not mean there is really a big market out there for them. Look at everything you do from a detached point of view. If you can separate fact from fiction, you're on your way to success in niche marketing.

List of Hot, In-Demand Niches Online

Finding that perfect niche can be a time-consuming process. You're going to have to do research and compare data from the different niches you've selected.

You've probably wondered to yourself, at least once, what you could do on the Internet that hasn't been done already. Just because most markets already have a business in them doesn't mean there isn't room for you to join in. Following is a list of some of the hottest, most in- demand niche markets you can enter.

Individualized presents: if you have a talent for some type

of art, whether it is drawing, sculpture, paint, creating, or any kind of variety of other skills, there is a market out there for distinct, custom gifts.

Market markets: whether you are looking to begin a business marketing items, or giving info or assistance, the group particular niches you can locate are substantial in number. There is constantly some special twist you can take into your technique that will certainly set you apart from the remainder, providing you a clientele that will keep going back to your website for their requirements. The possibilities in group specific niches are limitless, and always in demand.

Self-Help: self-help is just one of those things you can constantly earn money in. Whether you are aiming to assist individuals improve their dating skills, their connections, their physical appearance, or their education and learning, you will locate a hot market available for your service. Self-help is among those locations where growth just doesn't appear to be reducing.

Specialized product and services: there is always going to be a person around seeking something they can't find. Here is where you can discover a niche to fulfill the unusual demands of customers or businesses. Whether it is writing, shows, an item of some type, or whatever else they might need, your can-do perspective will offer you well in this niche market.

Discovering the right specific niche for you is absolutely going to be based a lot on your own research and also data. It is important to remember that your favorite hobby may not be in demand online, and so starting a business around that hobby would not be wise. Rather, be willing to compromise.

Enable yourself to consider the most successful locations, as in the checklist over, and after that use caution to choose the one that you feel matches your mentality or passion.

You'll find that the monetary rewards of selecting a lucrative endeavor will be greater than effectively compensate you for the compromise you may have made.

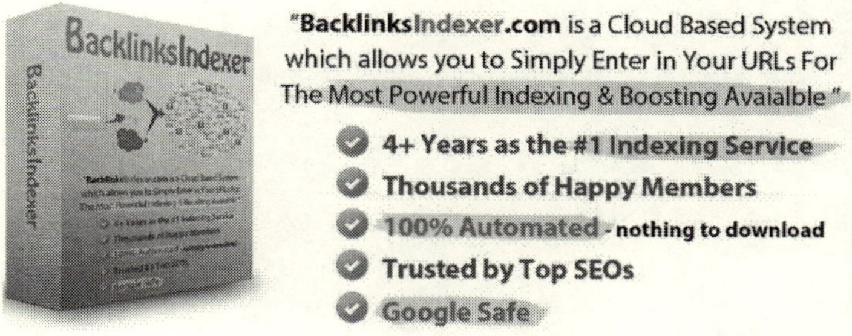

Backlinkindexer.com

https://bit.ly/2k3L4oM

4
SELLING PRODUCTS ONLINE

"The Art of Turning Your Offers into Money!"

Marketing Products on the Net

Marketing products on the Internet is one of the initial points that comes to mind when an individual decides about taking their business online. Virtually all of them have actually created a web site from which they market several of their products to consumers in much the exact same means they would at one of their retail outlets.

The possibilities here are basically unlimited, and also new possibilities arise constantly with the development of brand-new customer requirements. What is very important to note concerning selling products online is that you may not know just how many things are considered to be items. Believe for a moment regarding this: if it can be sold, it is possibly considered a product. So, with that in mind, you can customize your business around practically anything you would like to offer. The success or failing of your venture will depend on exactly how well you investigated the possibilities because market, and also some of it might even depend on luck.

The categories of items you can offer are fantastic in number. You can market whatever from software application to candle lights over the Internet. Some items, particularly perishables such as food, are not particularly well suited to internet marketing, however some have actually had success despite having those limitations.

There are benefits to selling products online. Second, while this might transform in the future, at this time you generally do not have to bill tax on some products you market in certain locations. The costs of running an online organisation are generally a lot lower and you will most likely need far less people on pay-roll, if any kind of at all.

The kind of products you decide to offer online will depend mainly on your personal interests and knowledge, as well as additionally on the outcomes of the research you perform to find out what will offer. Do not get distressed if the first few markets you look at are saturated already.

Types of Products You Can Offer Online

Selling products online is an interesting and also a very rewarding means to enter into business. Taking into consideration the huge variety of Internet users as well as the fact that this number is expanding, you make sure to locate a market for nearly anything you would love to offer. The chances being what they are, take a look at a few of one of the most common categories for products sold on the internet.

And possibly most typical, is the huge selection of goods you can find in simply any type of retail store in the country. Products such as books, sweet, shoes and also garments, electronics, software application, sporting products, they're all available for purchase online currently.

If somebody else is earning money on selling these products online, you can possibly get to do the same as well, given there suffices need to support the addition of your business to those already in operation.

You can also market items online called Resale Rights items. These are typically such things as insightful e-books as well as occasionally even software that another person has actually established and placed up for sale on the Internet.

If you choose to check into this sort of product selling, you will certainly require to be aware of exactly how it works prior to you jumping in. The most effective advice I can give when you consider re-selling is to ensure you know the provisions the initial seller has for the rights of resale. These can be located with the product, and also should be followed according to the product-maker's instructions.

Freelancers are products too, and also they are a large piece of the e-commerce market. When I refer to professional solutions, I'm talking about every little thing from the work-at-home solutions to the writing of customized programs for a business. It is such a wide area of chances that it would certainly be difficult to list, at the very least in this chapter, every one of the ways you can sell services online.

Keep in mind that many of these services will certainly require you to have at least some kind of expertise or special abilities, or possibly some other ability that the client requires for the project they are seeking. The freelancing field can conveniently be one of the most rewarding online businesses for you to begin.

Put simply, if it can be offered, and also if there is a

demand on the Internet for it, you can start a service with it. Just as a word of care, there are some points you may not have the ability to market online as an issue of regulation or licensing.

It is best, when conducting your study, to consult the appropriate professionals about the legality of what you want to offer. It is far better to locate this out before you offer something online than after you have actually marketed it.

Digital Products

Electronic book: Archetype of an electronic product. E-books exists only in digital format therefore there is no physical attributes such as that of touch, feel and scent.

Digital products use an additional interesting opportunity for you to offer products online. Thanks to the computer system and also ever- progressing technologies, this new form of product is hugely prominent since it is so easy to manage and move. Don't be misinterpreted by the name; electronic items does not refer to things such as electronic cams and video cameras, or anything else like that with words 'digital' in the name. Those are physical items. Digital items refers to the wide variety of products on the Internet that have no physical kind, and exist only as electronic info.

One of the most typical electronic products readily available on the Internet is software program. A terrific instance of a digital software application item you may have to pay for is anti-virus. You hear about a terrific brand-new anti-virus program on the market, go to the firm's site, pay for the item as well as download it rather than obtaining the disc for it from the shop.

An additional common sort of electronic item is all about entertainment. You can go online as well as download and install anything from video games to music to movies from the internet site of your choice. It is coming to be much more typical, for a number of reasons, that you will certainly be spending for this sort of digital item.

Another preferred sort of digital item we ought to talk about is the category known as electronic books as well as e-docs. Generally this group covers created material that is available digitally for you to download. Interesting opportunities have actually developed in this team because of the method of selling Resale Rights. When an author develops an e-book, he or she will certainly include what conditions apply to the resale of that written work. When another person acquires the product, that person is licensed to resell the work in accordance with the regards to the author's Resale Rights license. There are unbelievable opportunities for a person to make money in this fashion, either as the author or as the reseller.

Digital products also carry certain restrictions and rules as to how you may sell them online. Such things as intellectual property laws and copyright infringement laws prohibit certain practices in the sale of digital products.

Physical Products

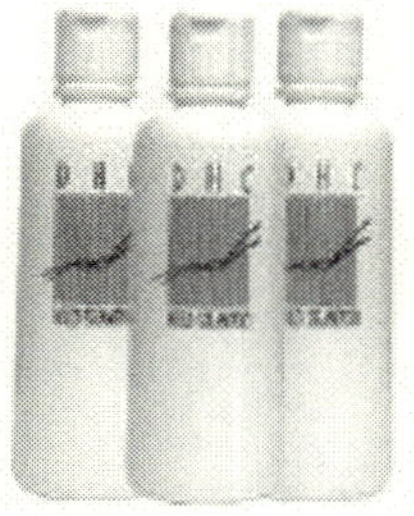

Shampoo: Instance of a physical product. You can touch, really feel and also smell.

Physical products make up a huge share of business volume that is performed on the internet daily. Whether the items are being sold retail or wholesale, physical items remain in high need and everybody is constantly around searching for a much better offer. There are a lot of means these products can be sold, and also, coupled with the variety of items available, you can create a company plan unlike anyone else's for marketing your physical products online.

If you really want to get a good idea of just what it means to have an unlimited variety of products to choose from for online sale, here's what you need to do. Once there, look in the business pages of the phone book for any and all sort of retailer, or other type of business where you know physical products will be sold. You may be saying to yourself that there are going to be similar products in many of the stores.

There are some things to know prior to you get into offering physical items online. Initially, you're most likely to need to understand every little thing you can concerning the items you are trying to market. You're going to need to find a place to put them. Unless you are using a drop-shipper, where you take the orders however a third party handles the inventory, you're possibly going to need a storage facility. This will depend upon the type of product you intend to market, and additionally on just how much inventory you are planning to stock.

Another consideration to make when marketing physical products online is shipping. Sometimes this makes physical products more expensive online than at a store. Just how do the products need to be packed for shipping?

Some things are sensitive to specific temperature levels, and this will certainly be very important for your shipping needs.

Physical products are great items to sell on the Internet. For the majority of physical products, there is an opportunity for a successful business waiting for you online.

Physical Product vs. Digital Product - Pros & Cons

Now, opportunities are that you have actually considered many different methods you could begin an organisation online, and you have actually probably also thought of great deals of different services or products that you can provide to customers. Below we will go over the items you can use to serve customers within these areas and the advantages and disadvantages of each.

You can offer detailed descriptions of the products you are selling, along with a gallery of pictures for those items. Many online buyers like to browse through the selection of items on a website, and they are often tempted to buy online simply because the costs of selling physical products online can be much lower than at a retail store.

On the other hand, physical items do have their drawbacks also. Some of the products you could offer online will be more affordable, however due to their size or weight, these items might set you back far way too much to deliver independently, and so the price to the client is much better if they purchase that item at the shop, in person.

Another consideration with physical products is that they can be perishable items. Physical products must be stored, so you will incur costs as a business for a location at which you can store your inventory until it is sold.

The advantage of selling digital products online is that you have no need for storage space. These conveniences are hard to ignore when choosing the products, you will sell.

Don't think you've found the holy grail of products because of these advantages. Digital products are prone to a few unique problems. You will need a plan for your Internet service that allows you a much higher bandwidth usage if you plan to sell digital products.

Knowing these advantages and disadvantages can assist you to choose which items you like. Simply know that the competitors for every kind of product can be intense, and so research study of your own will certainly still offer you the very best insight on your selections.

PROFIT BUILDER SOFTWARE - PROFESSIONAL

https://bit.ly/2jZeYdE

5
COPYWRITING

"How to Sell Your Product And Services in Writing!"

Salesmanship in Print

It is essential in any online endeavour that you develop a plan to market your site and your items to the world. Without advertising, it is rather most likely that no one will ever even understand that your site exists, and the repercussions of that are obvious. You will make couple of if any sales, and your venture will most likely stop working.

However there are tools you can use very successfully to market your company and get sales increasing quickly. Which tools you use and how you decide to use them will depend on numerous things. However no matter what you decide, there is one essential for the marketing campaign of your online service.

It's called copywriting.

History Fact: For anybody not knowledgeable about

copywriting, it is frequently referred to as "salesmanship in print". John E. Kennedy, a Canadian law enforcement officer, called it "salesmanship in print" in 1905, which label has actually adhered to it since. Copywriting is an essential tool for Web marketing, not to mention any other form of company marketing. The reasons are numerous, and the outcomes are difficult to overlook.

Among the greatest aspects of copywriting is that it is an affordable type of recurring advertising. Repeating is vital to the success of a marketing technique, because you wish to reach as many individuals as you can, as many times as you can.

It is, after all, the repetition that causes consumers to remember your product and to think of it first when they decide to make a purchase. You can work out several different articles that have related messages, all describing the products you are selling.

Thanks to the benefits provided by e-mail, you can easily send your articles to all of your consumers at whatever frequency you feel appropriate. Over and over again they will be reminded of the item you are selling. Some will be convinced to purchase from you, while others were not intending to buy up until you encouraged them they required the item, and they will purchase from you.

Salesmanship in print is a reminder that, while you are not verbally delivering a sales pitch to a customer in person or over the phone, you are still pitching your product. Because of its form, copywriting allows you to do just that.

Why is Copywriting Important?

The value of good copywriting for your online organisation can not be overstated. This is the single crucial piece of your marketing project. You are not just marketing your products. Bear in mind that you are likewise marketing your business. The items you offer may be found elsewhere. Possibilities are that they can be discovered in lots of locations. What you actually can't replace is your business. It is the only one by name and location, and individuals will prevent it for a number of reasons. Copy is what keeps this terrible circumstance from occurring.

To begin with, what is so important about effective copywriting is that it is your first impression on the Internet. Chances are it will be with copy when you contact a customer for the very first time. And if not, they will still run into the copy from your website when they start to try to find info on what you use. Either way, this is the first chance the client will have to see simply what type of company yours is, and it will be your first, and perhaps your only, possibility to show that you are worthy of that consumer's service. This is your opportunity not just to pitch your item to the client, however likewise to show the worthiness of your company as a professional in the field. That trust will not come again, so you have to make it the first time.

You will want to know how to effectively write the copy. Remember that the customer doesn't know who you are yet, so you're going to need to include the who, what, where, when, why, and how of your business and product in the copy that you write. If any of these elements is missing, or if the grammar is wrong, the customer may either be misled by something he or she reads, or perhaps the customer will just not trust what you have to say.

There is one more thing to be aware of: it is not enough that the copy you send to your customers be accurate and informative. It makes your message easier to read, and many will appreciate that.

Putting it all together will take a little work and study, but it's worth the effort. Reliable copywriting is plainly such an important element of your Online marketing that you can't manage to do without it. When the money begins rolling in, you'll be glad you took the time to do the copywriting well.

Copywriting: Composing the Perfect Heading

With lots of forms of writing you might find yourself without a title up until the work is total. Lots of authors make the title the last item of company for their work.

However, when you compose copy it works a little differently.

Most of the time you develop the heading as a guide for what you are going to write about, and it will function as a pointer throughout the short article of what message you plan to make clear to the reader. Headlines are very important, not only to catch the reader's attention, however also to improve your results with the online search engine. Let's have a look at what you need to do to develop the perfect heading.

One of the most helpful strategies for coming up with the perfect headline is to brainstorm. Think about the product or service you will be writing about, and who will likely be reading what you have written.

Scratch out the ones that obviously won't help. You may even find that a couple different headlines could be merged together to make a better headline.

By this point you must have your list worked down to just a handful of actually excellent prospects. Have a look at them one more time. Ask yourself these questions:

Does the headline capture my attention?

Is the headline plainly stated?

What words could I improve to get that critical greater online search engine rank?

Ask these concerns of each of the remaining headline choices.

Pointer: try to find a resource that will assist you by providing better words to say what you mean. There are lists of literally thousands of popular search words on the Internet. From this list you will have the ability to choose replacement words for your heading that will get you into more searches. Rewrite your headings appropriately.

As soon as you've done all of this you will have a list of great headings to pick from. If you only require to write one post, then select one of these that best matches what you require to state. Nevertheless, you are most likely to require numerous headings.

The others on your list might work as they are, or they could be modified a bit.

The point is that, although this appears like a great deal of fuss over a few words, it is the heading that promotes your work on the Internet. No other part of what you compose is so vital in making your work visible. And, as you know, if you can't discover a method to get observed on the Internet, you're as good as out of business.

Copywriting: Composing the Intro

His or her attention was obviously grabbed by that perfect headline you wrote if a reader has made it to the introduction segment of your article. But you do not desire that to be where their interest ends. Therefore, it is now your job to establish a well-written and interesting intro that will encourage the reader to go on. With the reader, you should be there every action of the way promoting him or her to go a little additional. Attention, like time, is a valuable thing finest not lost. That's why it's so simple to lose the attention of the reader. The reader will think of better ways to spend that time and will dismiss the rest of what you wrote if interest isn't sparked and fuelled.

At this point you have already succeeded at giving the reader a glimpse into the subject matter. It does not need to be restated word for word. The general idea here is to let the readers know that the headline was not just to reel them in.

It's often a good idea to enlist the reader's attention a little further by saying something like "picture this" or "imagine if". You are encouraging the reader to not just read, but to actively participate in this article. The benefit to you as the copywriter is that you are engaging the reader fully and you are thereby quite likely to keep him or her reading to the end.

Finally comes a point of great importance in any form of writing. Do not forget that you are supposed to be introducing something when you are preparing the introduction to the rest of your work. That's where the final sentence of the paragraph comes in. It should not only be a transition into the next paragraph, but also a declaration of what is to come. It is quite helpful to the reader to know where this is all leading to.

To do this effectively, the final sentence of the introduction should be a brief statement of either the points you intend to make, or a suggestion that you are about to dive further into the subject. No matter how you do it, this transition must be smooth or it will disrupt the flow of your writing.

Writing the introduction is really just the next step in a process. You'll find that the introduction, written effectively, can help you to make it through the rest of your work with ease and speed.

Copywriting: Body and Conclusion

Once you've finished the introduction to the article, you're well on your way. It may seem to you as though you still have most of the work left to do, but the hardest part is finished.

Writing the body of the article will take a little step-by-step organization. Now all you have to do is fill in the blanks if you outlined your steps in the introduction. Use clear, easy to read language. Be careful not to trail off on one point too much. Remember, this is most-likely going to be a short work of only a few hundred words or so. So it's important not to rob from one point to overdo another.

As you work through the body of the paper, keep in mind that separate points will need to be in separate paragraphs for emphasis. Jumping from one key point to another without the paragraph changing will make it harder for the reader to keep up, and some of what you wrote might be missed when read. Keeping the writing easy for you, will keep the reading easy for the customer.

Once you've completed all of the body, you have the conclusion to work on. Once you've summarized you can make a final pitch to the reader. Whatever your goal in this article, here is your final chance to make the sale.

Now you need to do just a few more things before this article is ready. The first is to run a spelling and grammar check on what you've written. Be sure it sounds to you now like it sounded when you wrote it.

Once any revisions are completed, you're finished. By this point you've gone through the whole process and you should be confident with your work. Consider having someone else read it and get that person's opinion if you're not. When it's read by your customers, there's no harm in a little more revision if it will make the work you've done that much more effective.

Copywriting: Publishing Your Work

Okay, so you have this article you've written, and you're convinced that it's going to bring in tons of new leads to your site and boost profits like nothing else has done before. That's great, but how do you get the article to readers in the first place?

The first place you will want to publish your article is on your own website. Publishing your articles on your own site will allow for the search engines to link searcher directly to your site.

If you have an opt-in list, and you should, you can make use of it for publishing your articles. All it takes is one e-mail to spread the message of your article to the potentially thousands of people on your opt-in list. Not only does it entice them, it entertains them if you wrote your copy well.

One of the easiest options you have is to go online and search for affiliate marketers. They have access to all of the sites that will publish your work on their site, with a link back to yours. At any rate, this is a highly effective tool to spread your message and reel in the customers.

These are just the major ways for you to publish your copy on the Internet. There are other options as well, and you can research those to decide if they will help you. In any case, publishing your work on the Internet is a relatively painless and fast process that brings in more leads, perhaps, than any other method of Internet Marketing advertisement.

Copywriting: Planning Your Message

As I mentioned before, copywriting is your first impression to the customer, and it can be a make or break proposition. With that in mind, there are some things that need to be discussed about preparing before you begin your copywriting work.

The very first thing you must do if you plan to write an effective article about your company and it's products is get to know the products as completely as you possibly can. This means getting to know all of its advantages, disadvantages, who in the market is going to want this product or need, what they intend to use the product for, etc. It may seem silly to you at first, but you really will be surprised when you get to know all the things about a product that you can't tell just by looking at it.

Once you have enough information on the product, and on the business too, you're next step will be getting to know the consumer better. What are the demographics in this market? What makes these customers want or need this product? How can you approach them and make that key first impression the best it can be? These are all things you must be able to find out before you start communicating your message. The customers will have their own ideas and values, and it is up to you as the copywriter to hit the right chords with them to make them want to buy from your company. The alternative is that they go to the competition.

After you feel that you have gathered all the information you can from both the demand and the supply side of the market, it's time to put all the information together and plan your approach. This will take putting things in logical order so that you can paint yourself a clear picture of how the article should finish and start. A lot of what you do at this point with organization will depend on the unique circumstances of the product and the consumer.

Once you've finished the planning, you're ready to write. Now comes the interesting part. You will need to have a title that not only catches the reader's attention, but that also can achieve a high search engine ranking. You will need to put together an introduction for the article that will establish interest and make the reader want to keep going. You will then need to write an effective and informative body and conclusion that will give the consumer all the reasons he or she needs to justify the purchase. Finally you will need to publish the copy so customers will get the message.

A Short List of Words that Sell

It is not enough that you have used proper grammar and an effective tone in your work when you are copywriting. It is also not enough that you have made your work interesting, nor that you have fully described the product in detail and made the customer aware of all the benefits it offers. Yes, these and other factors are of great importance, but there is one more thing that will be the life of your work. This one factor is so important that, without using this, your work may never have any chance of getting to the multitude of customers you are trying to reach, and if it does, you may never motivate many of them to buy what you have to sell.

What you need is words that sell. Following are some of the words that sell, and why they do it.

Words such as powerful, durable, unbeatable, unstoppable, and incredible, are power words. These words establish the strength and the value of the subject. They are helpful in establishing a trust in the product.

Words like hurry and urgent, and phrases like don't wait, won't last, and act now, are all time-based and encourage the reader to move quickly. After all, the more time you spend on a decision, the more likely you are to change your mind and decide against what you were planning to do. A sense of urgency overcomes this obstacle to the sale.

Words that evoke thought, such as the words secret, interesting, and provocative are bait to catch your customer up and get him or her to read more.

There are also good words that make people see dollar signs. Words such as cheap, lowest price, most affordable, discount, profitable, lucrative, and earnings make people think about that almighty dollar. And what better bait to make the sale exists than the bait that makes people think about money?

This is by no means an all-inclusive list of words that sell. There are literally hundreds of power words that can catch the attention of a customer and lure them in for the sales pitch. These words, placed effectively throughout your article or other copy will give you just the edge you're looking for. Not only will they convince more readers of the need for your product, they are also the kind of words that get you to the top of the search engine rankings where you must be if you expect to be found in the first place.

Remember, if the customer can't find you in a short time, you don't stand a chance of being noticed. You have to be at the top of the list with the words that sell, or the rest of the words you wrote won't matter at all.

All-Time Attention Getting Headlines

Okay, so here's the clincher to the entire world of media. It doesn't matter whether it's a news article, a program on tv, an announcement on the radio, or copy on the Internet, it's got to have a title, or heading. The heading, regardless of the media kind, is the first thing you are likely to see. That said, it needs to be catchy. This is especially true on the Internet where one particular word in the headline may be why your copy shows up on a search, and after that the remainder of the headline catches the searcher's attention. It's such an essential aspect of the copywriting world that I've included here a list of attention grabbing headings to offer you a concept of what yours might need to seem like. Here they are:

Attempt to be Abundant!

7 Actions to Financial Freedom.
How $20 Spent May Conserve You $2,000.
How I Succeeded With a Fool Idea.
A $10,000 Error!
How to Rob Banks Lawfully.
The Secret to Being Wealthy.
How to Burn Off Body Fat, Hour-by-Hour.
What Your Attorney Doesn't Want You to Know Take This One Minute Test!
Why Wall Street Journal Readers Live Much Better.
How You Can Get a Quick Loan of $1,000.
Wish to Be a Legal Investigator?
How to Compose a Hit Song and Offer It.
Who is Making a Bundle and How.
Eliminate Money Concerns for Good.
The Truth About Getting Rich.
How I Enhanced My Memory in One Evening.
Free Book Tells You 12 Tricks of Better Lawn Care.

... And there are many more out there.

You might have observed that the majority of the chosen headlines were about money. Well, there's no mistake about that. Cash is among those things that tends to capture the attention of everyone. Have you ever been in a car park and saw cash on the pavement? You reach down to select it up, unfold it, and find that it is fake and has either a religious or inspirational message inside. It's similar to a heading. Mention something like money and everyone takes notice. And it's not just money; other words are catchy too. It simply takes knowing what you're advertising, and you can discover a way to make readers notice your heading.

While this list is by no means complete, I hope that it has offered you with some insight into what you ought to be looking for when writing your own headings.

6
SEARCH ENGINE OPTIMIZATION

"Discover How YOU-- Or Anybody-- Can Benefit From The Internet's Significant Search Engines And Their Terrific Traffic FREE of Charge And Build Your Websites Rankings Exponentially!"

What is Search Engine Optimization (SEO)?

Let's say you in a crowd of people waiting to see a celebrity. What did you see about the habits of the fans? What did you observe?

Chances are that in either of those situations you saw a huge crowd of people all combating to get to the front where they could be seen and heard. There is a great deal of shoving and pushing and yelling and all of that. It's turmoil, and many individuals would just as soon avoid such a scenario. It's all about competition. The few who get to the front of the crowd are the only ones who stand a chance to have their voices heard. It is these couple of people who will have the chance to gain the rewards of their effort.

So now you're asking yourself: "Simply what does all this pertain to SEO?" And the response is a basic one: competition.

Competitors in any field is the battle not only for survival however likewise for dominance. Very few desire to 'simply get by'.

Search Engine Optimization is really a technical science more than anything. It is the process of gathering details on your market and your rivals in an effort to great tune your website's headlines and material so that you attain more hits on every search a web-surfer carries out. It is up to you to make sure that your site has the best, and the most, of these popular search terms.

The way it works, generally, is by search engines tapping all the sites with the most plentiful and precise search terms appropriate to a search. When you utilize the ideal terms to describe the content of your website, you attain a higher ranking with that search engine. Customize your website as required so you can keep your rankings higher and remain ahead of the competition.

Why is Search Engine Optimization Important?

You have a lot to stress about when you start any company. However above all else, you need to concern yourself with exposure. If the consumer does not know you exist, how can you anticipate him or her to ever visit your business? In the real world, stores and other businesses have many ways of getting noticed. Radio, television, newspaper, and mailing advertisements are all ways that they get noticed.

However what about the individual taking a trip through the town where you do business? Possibilities are that the tourist will not have gotten any of these ads.

What else can you do to bring in these prospective consumers? And the response is your signs. The signs you position are a clear beacon to the customer of where you are. You see it all the time, driving down the highway. And the bigger the indication, the better it catches your attention.

It actually works rather the same way with SEO. You need to be observed. The best way for you to get observed is to have, figuratively speaking, the most significant and the very best indication. That's how traffic on the Internet, zipping by, notices that you even exist. It's the words you use and how you use them to describe your site and its material that get you the customers.

This is where it ends up being so important to utilize SEO to your benefit. If you can create that critical list of best keywords to explain your site, and if you can integrate those words into the content of your site, then you stand far greater possibilities of directing that Internet traffic to you instead of your competitors. Remember, if you do not get the customers, they will.

It doesn't cost you anything to appear on an online search engine's results. But it can cost you everything if you do not show up on a search. The quantity of revenue you have prepared for your company is going to depend on how well you can use this function of Online marketing. If you can't get the consumers to observe you, you might as well throw those revenue objectives in the fireplace.

The traffic on the Internet is much pickier than the traffic on the streets. It is focused traffic, looking for a particular require or want. They will browse, discover, and buy. Who they buy from is of little significance to them, however to you, it is whatever. So when you consider why it is very important to successfully use search engine optimization, simply remember that everybody on the Internet is really a traveler through your town, and if you don't have that sign they'll observe, they're going to pass you by.

Actions for Search Engine Optimization (SEO)

Search Engine Optimization, or merely SEO, is a rather involved procedure that you must follow through to ensure that your Internet business is getting results and revenues. This is the most crucial methods by which you can direct traffic to your website, and so it is critically essential that you comprehend at least the basic actions in the process to enhance your ranking with the search engines.

1. Know your competition. Perform searches to gather information. Repeat this process frequently, using up-to-date search terms.

2. You can go online and acquire huge lists of keywords that are used all the time. Put together the list according to the words that will have the many impact on your website.

3. Find methods to combine the keywords you have actually selected. The more combinations you can incorporate into the content of your site, the better will be your results.

4. Modify the material of your website. Modification headings, labels, and content throughout your website to enhance the abilities of your website to draw in highly-directed traffic.

5. Fine-tune your keyword list frequently. Knowing that the Internet is ever-evolving, you need to remain on top of what words will have the most impact.

6. Make sure that your URL is added to the top search engines. Know which search engines are most popular.

7. Keep track of your results. Just like grades in school, the rankings you attain will tell you how well you're doing and just how much you need to improve for that A+. Evaluate whatever details you can collect and continuously work to enhance your outcomes.

8. Repeat the process. Over and over once again, you will need to redo all of these actions, bearing in mind that the competition is doing the very same. Constantly search for ingenious methods to improve your outcomes. Sticking to the same old stuff all the time is not how giants are made.

This is a fairly fundamental illustration of the process you need to follow to optimize your search engine results. There are certainly more methods to fine-tune your site's rankings.

However, for the sake of beginning, this list ought to serve to put you on the path towards greater online search engine rankings, and greater business incomes.

Pursuing the Competitors With SEO

No matter what company you remain in, there is one common element all services share: they have competitors. Sure, the exception is the monopoly, but you would be hard-pressed to find any type of true monopoly on the Internet. More likely you will find that there are at least a few, and perhaps as many as hundreds, of rivals all scrambling to get to the top. If you have an Internet service, you are among them. And for you to be successful, you should understand how to effectively compete. It's a game with very genuine consequences, and winning is the ultimate goal.

Search Engine Optimization is one way you can effectively compete with others in your market. The only way you can even start to compete with them is to know them.

Search for all the sites you can find that may be doing the same thing you are, and then visit each one. When you go to each site, take notes on layout, content, obvious keywords, and any other things about the site that may make it more visible than yours in searches.

Once you've gotten through all of the sites and reviewed the results of your study, look for ways to enhance the quality of your own site. Consider different types of content, better or more keywords, and any other additions that will make your site as good or better than the competition.

Besides wanting to others for concepts, also think about ways you can improve your website that others have actually not tried. Development is what will set you above the rest. It does not injured to include an innovation to your site to check the marketplace's action. Just make certain to study it for effectiveness before you use it. You wish to be reasonable sure that it will work before you put the concept to the test.

A final note: constantly examine your results. Determine what worked and what did not work. Watch on your competition for what they are doing. This is an ongoing procedure without end. It is the very best way to pursue the competition online, and it will be the key to your success or failure.

Building a Content-Rich Website

In order for your efforts to enhance your search engine results to work, you will require to make your whole website a signboard of sorts. Everywhere you can place some keyword to effectively construct your online search engine rankings, you must. This is the best method for you to get your service discovered on the Internet. The more individuals who search for what you sell, the more customers you will likely have.

What are they going to do when they get to your site? That's why it's so important that you make not just a noticeable site, but also it must be a content-rich site.

It is up to you as the Internet Marketer and business owner to develop content rich in information that will not only attract people to your site, but keep them there long enough for you to make the sale. In the case of Internet business where information is the only thing your site offers, you really need to keep up on this.

The best methods to make yours a content-rich site involve a lot of writing. You require to write articles that will notify and captivate readers. These posts should be associated with your website's market. The more little articles you discuss various different aspects of the subject of your website, the better. Another thing that produces a content-rich website is news. Details associating with some brand-new occasion in the market will considerably improve the material of your website. Even interviews, reports, and product descriptions can enhance content.

The last thing to remember is that your content should be revised frequently. The usual details will wear, so you have to be on top of it, with something new all the time.

Also, remember that the keywords are how you actually get observed. The more material you have, the more room you have actually got for the essential keywords. When you include material, make certain to have as lots of keywords as you can incorporated into that content. It's everything about getting noticed and getting results, and keywords and content are how you get there.

7
LEVERAGING ON AFFILIATE PROGRAMS

"How to Get an Army of Merchants to Willingly Assist You Market Your Product or Service All Over The Internet!"

What is an Affiliate Program?

Have you ever heard the old stating "There's strength in numbers"? Or how about he recommendation that people "team together"? There are numerous other ways to state the same thing. And what that 'thing' we're describing is the concept that more people or companies can get more work achieved if they integrate their efforts. It's a reliable technique to success in any venture, and it has actually even proven itself in the world of Web marketing. Online, this concept is known as an affiliate program.

Affiliate programs, otherwise referred to as bounty programs, associate programs, or referral programs, are collaborations in between you and an online merchant where you supply an ad or some other link to the merchant's website. When you recommend this merchant's website, or in some other way provide an endorsement, you earn a fee for your referral. Depending on the type of affiliate program you are joining, and the terms to the program, you might make your commission either for purchases made by your referral or just for leads generated, or from both.

If you are a merchant, it is to your advantage to join an affiliate program since you are increasing the visibility of your product on the Internet. Successfully putting affiliate advertisements on the websites of your affiliates will provide you possibly thousands of brand-new visitors.

For the online company that is not providing anything for sale, however rather just information of some sort, affiliate programs might quickly become the life-blood of your company. If all you are giving visitors to your site is entertaining or helpful material, and you don't charge for it, then you will require to have some other method to attract earnings. Affiliate programs offer you simply that possibility. You can join an affiliate program and start putting ads on your website. Make sure that the advertisements relate to the customers who are visiting your site. If it is crucial to them, they will be more likely to click the link. The more clicks, the more referrals. The more recommendations, the more money you make. It's really a sensible and extremely simple process.

In the competitive landscape of e-commerce, you must discover an edge to get you the incomes you're going for. Affiliate programs provide a hassle-free, basic, and hugely efficient way to gain that edge. They truly are a vital money maker for any online business.

Why Use Affiliate Programs?

There is so much reading and research study that goes into the development of a sound online business method that some people might give up before they get going. It's the affiliate program, and I'm going to tell you why it is such a great idea.

This part is for the online merchant selling products or services. Whether you've been in business online for awhile, or if you're just starting, you will require to produce traffic for your website to build sales. Affiliate programs group together literally countless merchants and non-merchants alike, all searching for the same thing: traffic. The way it works for you as the merchant is this: you join an affiliate program, others sign up with and advertise your site in some way on their website. You get highly-interested leads from them, and you pay them for it. The terrific feature of the programs is that they are pay- for-performance. You do not pay unless a sale or a lead is generated from that affiliate. Bear in mind that the non- merchant wishes to make as numerous recommendations as possible, so they will actually be working for both their, and your, benefit.

For the non-merchant business there stand out benefits to signing up with an affiliate. First, you will be supplying your visitors with links to the merchant, so you generate income by getting more individuals to come to your website, and after that getting them to go to the merchant. You earn money for the number of sales or leads created by your efforts. Another thing to bear in mind is that you have the opportunity to increase this traffic by getting others to advertise your site. Real, you will have to pay for the leads generated, but the benefits of that included traffic to your site far outweigh the costs.

As a final note to all online services, affiliate programs are reasonably simple and inexpensive to handle. They remain in the business of generating company for all of their clients. Therefore, it is usually far less costly, and much less work for you to join an affiliate program than it would be for you to attempt to manage your own list of affiliates. And with the massive variety of members these affiliate programs have, you remain in a position to tap a far larger range of the market than you could hope for if you do the entire thing on your own.

How to Establish an Affiliate Program for Your Products

You're going to need an effective strategy to advertise what you have for sale when it comes to marketing your products. Signing up with an affiliate program is certainly among the very best methods to accomplish this. Nevertheless, you may currently be in business and, for one factor or another, you've chosen that you would rather do the affiliating by yourself. Or, if you're just getting started, you might have the independent spirit that informs you to do it on your own or not to do it at all. In either case, you can start your own affiliate program to market your items on the Internet. Let's take a look at how it can be done.

The first thing you will require to do is choose what sites out there will offer the type of traffic that would wish to buy what you're selling. You wouldn't want to contact a website that discusses pets if your in business selling power tools. This simply wouldn't be an excellent option as an affiliate marketer. You would be far much better off selecting sites whose topic is comparable to your product. A website talking about mechanics, or construction, would be a far much better lead for you to follow. It's all about matching like for like and producing a list of possible affiliate online marketers.

When you have your list, you will need to establish a strong sales letter to send out the webmaster of each site. When you do this, be sure to consist of all of the selling points for your proposal, and info on what commission you are offering for sales generated by them. Check the letter thoroughly, as this is your one possibility for a good impression. Send the letters out.

Once you have actually signed on some affiliate marketers, you'll require affiliate software to keep track of the sales generated, and how much commission you require to pay.

Then you will be responsible for cutting the commission checks and sending them out. An option to handling all of this yourself is to enlist the services of a third-party affiliate tracker. This company will handle the tracking of sales and the distribution of commissions for you. Either alternative will work.

No matter which way you pick, running your own affiliate marketing operation to sell your items will give you the control over where and how the ads are positioned, and over who will be directing traffic to your website. Be aware, however, that this is more work than having an affiliate program run it for you. However if you know what you want, this is how it's done.

Recommended Affiliate Programs

There are thousands of affiliate marketing programs online that can do the affiliate marketing for you. Just to get you started here is a good list of affiliate programs that I recommend you consider:

- http://paydotcom.com/
- http://www.clickbank.com/
- http://www.jvmanager.com/
- http://www.forex-affiliate.com/
- http://www.pokeraffiliate.com/
- http://www.clickbooth.com/
- https://www.cafepress.com/

- http://www.credit.com/
- http://platinumpartner.com/
- http://www.leadflash.com/
- -http://www.studentloanconsolidator.com/
- http://www.e-gold.com/
- http://www.wholesaleriches.com/
- http://www.earnunited.com/
- http://www.lunarpages.com/
- http://genbucks.com/

As you look through the list and visit these sites, be sure to note what their minimum payout is, and what type of service they offer. Depending on the needs of your business, one of these may be the best fit for you.

How to Employ Affiliates

If you have actually decided to go your own way and begin not only your own online service, but also your own affiliate program, you have actually got a great deal of work to do. It's a comprehensive process with many things to do, and numerous things to bear in mind. But, if you're aiming to become successful in e- commerce, this is one terrific way to do it.

In this first section on recruiting affiliates, I want to make you aware of the legwork you'll need to do before you even get up and running. Go through and make sure that everything is in the correct place.

Spell check each page of the website to make certain whatever is as it ought to be. The last thing you desire is for somebody to take a look at your website and be instantly switched off by basic errors you have actually neglected to fix. Your site will require to be top-shelf.

You'll need to do some searching once you've gone through and corrected all the errors. Find all of the affiliate directories you can and list them. These are the sites you will require to go to for details and links to the affiliate programs in the classification where you want to be listed. You may be asking why you would wish to do this. Well, it's easy. You want to be listed in as many places as you can, due to the fact that others will come searching for affiliates and most likely stumble upon your website in their search. Most of the affiliate programs directory sites out there will think about putting a free link to your program on their website. Therefore, it is to your benefit to understand what the others are doing so you can be as great or better than they are.

Create an affiliate information page on your site. If you go to any of the affiliate programs on your list you will probably find this type of page.

By now you're ready to make your carry on to the next action. That next step will be deciding what kind of strategy you will use. We'll go over plans in Part 2.

When you remain in business of hiring affiliates, you require to understand that some affiliates have actually been doing this for awhile and they know what they're trying to find, and what they're not. The kind of plan you decide to use when you pay your affiliates will identify, oftentimes, who will come to you and who will not.

There are 3 major plan types for you to consider. However, there are also tiers. We'll start with the strategies, then move into a conversation on tiers.

Pay-Per-Click, or PPC, plans are the plans you might have heard the most about. This kind of affiliate strategy, just like the other two, is performance based. The way it works is easy. A visitor to a site sees a banner ad or some other link to a website. She or he clicks that link. Each click is worth a payment to the owner of that site. While this is a terrific method to go, there has been some issue just recently about "click fraud" where clicks are being created with the sole goal of getting more cash for the host site.

Pay-Per-Sale, or PPS, plans enable more discretion. When a sale is made, with this type of plan the merchant only pays the commission to the affiliate. Whatever the commission is, the merchant pays based upon the cost of the merchandise sold.

Pay-Per-Lead, or PPL, is the last kind of commission plan. With this strategy the merchant will pay the commission to the affiliate whenever a lead is produced.

This may happen either from directed traffic that concerns the merchant's website and register for something, or in some other method can be thought about as a 'lead'.

Now let's take a look at tiers. The way tiers work is pretty easy as well. It's all about recommendations. Let's state you set up 2 tiers. The first tier is affiliates who came directly to you. They will get commission not just on the traffic they send out to you, but likewise on the traffic their referrals send as well. The second tier is affiliates who were described you through another affiliate. These get commission on their directed traffic, and the first tier affiliate gets a smaller sized commission as well, with not work done on his/her part.

When you decide to set up an affiliate plan, these are the primary options you have. You can work out the information however you like. Simply bear in mind that the main point is whether your plan will be competitive and for that reason worth the affiliates time to join up.

Now you're at the final stretch in the process of recruiting affiliates. You will want to be constantly reworking your strategy and improving upon deficiencies so that your affiliate program will be a success.

When you go to the directory site's site, bear in mind that each of the directory sites will have different requirements. There will likewise be some (really couple of) types of sites they will decline ever. The main things all of these directories will be requesting for is the URL for your site, the plan you plan to utilize for payment, and a description of your website and the services you will use. Remember that these submissions will be reviewed carefully therefore it is to your benefit to be thorough and truthful.

You will need to place your advertisements on someone else's site. The point is that this, too, is a business. You want to get people involved as affiliates, so you must advertise.

Lastly, as with all strategies, it is not enough simply to make the plan and put it into action. What if something in your strategy did not work well? How will you know?

This is why you will require to continuously review the outcomes of your strategy to determine what is working and what is not. Act on it immediately when you come across something that could be improved. The more you do this, the more reliable your recruiting will become. Over and over again you will develop your system to end up being more competitive, and the revenues from your efforts will increase, especially if you are doing this in conjunction with merchandising on your site.

Although this procedure covered 3 articles, you need to know that there is constantly more out there on this subject. No matter how quickly you move online, you will constantly have some catching up to do. So keep studying the subject beyond what you've checked out to continue perfecting your affiliate hiring efforts.

Signing Up With Affiliate Programs to Increase Your Earnings Streams

You have a website where you operate a successful business. There is one great thing you can do to increase revenues: multiply your income streams by joining affiliate programs. This is the best way for you to increase the income generated by your online business without really adding any work.

The first thing for you to consider is the market you remain in. When you go to an affiliate program to join, you will be advertising other's businesses on your site.

So, in order for you to make the most cash off each advertisement, you require to select the business most appropriate for the traffic on your website. The visitors to your site must be interested in what you are promoting or they will not click the link. Remember that the affiliate programs work on a pay- for-performance basis, so the more traffic you can direct through those links, the more money you make.

Consider how you could rearrange the area on the numerous pages of your site. If you wish to place banner ads on your site, this is going to be very important. Likewise, I would extremely advise that you avoid pop-up advertisements or other invasive techniques. These are frequently more of an inconvenience to visitors and may even drive them away. I personally prevent numerous websites precisely for this reason. However, at any rate, think about how you might make better use of the space on your site to put highly noticeable advertisements for your clients to see.

Know the affiliate program's policies. Such considerations

as their performance in distributing commissions to affiliates should be of great concern to you. Always be ready to make changes to your site to enhance not only your existing revenue streams, but also the revenue generated from your status as an affiliate.

To do this you require to keep your site full and content-rich of factors for your customers to keep coming back for more. No matter what your site is about, or how else you make your cash, joining an affiliate program is a terrific, virtually work- totally free way to increase your earnings streams. After all, who in their right mind would decline an easy way to get more cash?

What to Look for in an Affiliate Program before Signing Up With

Affiliate programs offer you a very rewarding and unique opportunity to make money. Don't go jumping into the first affiliate program you find.

The first thing to take a look at in an affiliate program is who it deals with. Some of the affiliate programs are very particular in their customers, such as gaming, sports, retail, wholesale, business-to-business, and etc. Make certain to choose those who are likely to have affiliates such as yourself.

Another thing to consider is the strategy the affiliate utilizes. Is it PPC, PPL, or PPS? Depending upon your goals, you might wish to select an affiliate program with a Particular pay plan. Also search for whether the program provides tiers. It will be to your benefit to acquire referrals to the program if they provide tiers, because you will make money off of your referrals' results in addition to your own performance.

Take note of the commission that is paid. Look around and see if the other programs are comparable. If you discover that one program pays 10% and another pays 30%, it would be ridiculous to choose the one that pays less.

On the subject of commissions, make certain you understand what the minimum payout is. Discover how they pay. Will they mail you a check, wire the money to you, utilize PayPal, or what? Likewise, make sure to inspect around and see if you discover any indicator that the program you are considering has a history of issues with commission payments. This would be a red flag to avoid that company.

Beyond these tips, the very best guidance I can give you is to utilize good judgment. When you are taking a look at these sites, think about other things that may be essential to you, and do not hesitate to submit concerns to a representative of the affiliate program. They want your company, and they'll enjoy to react when they can. As with all things in company, beware not to move too rapidly. It might be that you passed over some detail of significance, and if you jump in prematurely, you have actually slipped up. However if you take a little more time to consider the choice, you'll make the best choice and join a great affiliate program.

Places to Hunt for Rewarding Affiliate Programs

As opposed to the post on recommended affiliate programs, this post is mostly a list of locations where you can go to find the most gratifying affiliate programs to join. A few of these are affiliate programs in and of themselves, whereas others are the affiliate program directory sites I mentioned as soon as previously.

These are a terrific resource when you want to discover the very best program for you. They help to arrange the countless affiliate programs out there into a simple to navigate compilation. Here are the places to go:

- http://www.clickbank.com/

- http://paydotcom.com/
- http://www.commissionjunction.com/
- http://www.associateprograms.com/
- http://www.affiliatefirst.com/
- http://www.abestweb.com/
- http://www.affiliatetip.com/
- http://www.affiliateguide.com/
- http://simplythebest.net/affiliates/
- http://www.affiliate-programs-directory.com/
- http://www.affiliateseeking.com/
- http://www.globalhighway.com/
- http://www.2-tier.com/
- http://www.sponsordirectory.com/
- http://www.100best-affiliate-programs.com/

This list is just a portion of the directories out there where you can find affiliate programs that are perfect for you. When you look at some of these, you will notice that many of them list well over a thousand different programs. With that in mind, this list should give you plenty of options!

8
STRIKING JOINT VENTURE OFFERS

"It's Really Everything About Partnering for Success."

Why Joint Venture is the one of the best Free Marketing Approaches

People are scared of business offers going bad, so they tend to guide clear of any sort of joint venture. Unlike most joint endeavors, joint venture marketing does not need sharing of profits. Let me explain what makes joint venture marketing such a great method of free marketing.

The very first and probably most important factor is that it provides endorsements from other merchants and with recommendations comes trust. Not only are you expanding your client base to include your venture partner's customers but you will also be managed more trust from your venture partner's customers since he/she has endorsed you. And as soon as a merchant is considered credible they'll have a devoted consumer base for numerous, several years to come.

The second reason, as I just mentioned, is the expanded customer base that comes with joint ventures. I'm sure you can easily see how beneficial joint ventures can be.

The third factor joint venture marketing is great is the potential for more new clients. The very truth that you will be offering more service or products through your joint venture is very attractive to potential clients. The more you have to offer the more traffic you'll likely get.

And last, however definitely not least, is how this can affect your capability to draw in more potential joint venture partners to more broaden your service and consumer base. The same method that you use to start your initial joint venture can be used for future expansion. The greatest element of future joint venture expansion is the fact that a preliminary joint venture success makes you a more attractive potential partner for other highly successful merchants.

As you can see, joint venture marketing can most absolutely operate in your favor. The factors I've pointed out above are simply a few of lots of that can work to your advantage. And, the very best factor of all, it's all totally free.

Joint Venture in a Nutshell

Joint venture is best defined as two (or in numerous circumstances more than two) celebrations forming an alliance to boost sales and profits in their company. This form of collaboration pays for the celebrations to it lots of other benefits, as well, that make it an extremely appealing choice to lots of organisation people.

Joint venture it a method of marketing that involves entering into a partnership with another business for the purpose of each partner increasing profits. Such marketing methods do not make use of the priceless assets of good customer relationships and business credibility that are truly the essential elements of success in joint venture partnerships.

The concept of a joint venture is best for those who are attempting to target a particular niche market and there are other business who are currently doing business with them successfully. Developing a joint venture with one of these business would open that market up to you much quicker and with much greater results than if you tried to reach the market by yourself. It also permits you broad direct exposure to that market without investing all your hard-earned money on marketing.

There are numerous other advantages to joint ventures, too. You might be able to gain near-instant trustworthiness through leveraging on your partners excellent credibility.

There's a surefire boost in response to your sales message because your partner's consumers will be seeing it, as well. Not to mention the advantage of being able to provide your consumers products used by your venture partner. You earn money off of it while making your customers delighted by providing something brand-new to them.

As you can see there are so many ways that joint ventures are genuinely a win-win situation. You get essentially free advertising, inherit a recognized customer base, gain credibility from your partner's great credibility, extra items to offer to your consumers and utilize that will benefit both you and your partner. So really there's nothing but advantage that can originate from participating in a joint venture, as long as you select the right partner.

Composing Your Joint Venture Proposals

Your joint venture proposal is the key consider whether

you'll have a joint venture collaboration, or not. You need to compose a powerful, but not overwhelming, proposal.

You require to consist of all the key components of what might you an excellent potential partner, while not overdoing it. And most significantly, you require to make your potential partner wish to work with you. I've put together a list of all the components to an effective joint venture proposition and will share them with you.

The first ingredient to a winning joint venture proposal is to consist of everything that you might bring to the partnership that would benefit the other celebration. This is important, because after all, this is supposed to be an equally beneficial collaboration. You'll wish to tell them what you can do for them. Explain what your organisation can do to enhance their business and you'll have their attention.

The next essential element to an effective joint venture proposition is offer a complimentary sample of what you provide your customers. If you offer items offer your prospective partner a free sample or two. If you sell services, let them have a look at your work, or potentially read letters from satisfied clients. Make it simple for them to see why you 'd be a terrific company to partner with.

The most essential aspect of your proposal is your writing. Even if you're the best in your industry, if you can't communicate that in writing you're most likely to get lost in the shuffle. When writing your joint venture proposition you require to be clear, brief and concise. Express your interest in partnering with them. Discuss what you need to use and what they stand to acquire. Attempt not to consist of a lot of details in your preliminary proposition, however be sure to consist of a minimum of 2 ways of contact for them to reach you need to they want more information or have any questions.

If you follow the guidelines I've given you here you should have no trouble putting together a joint venture proposal. And in not time you should be well on your way to writing a successful joint venture proposal.

How to Try To Find Joint Venture Partners

Success is almost wholly dependent on the partner you choose when it comes to joint ventures. Choose the best partner and earnings and sales will come quickly and quickly. Pick the incorrect partner and failure is distinguished.

The key to picking the ideal joint venture partner is to do your research. I can not worry enough the value of checking out your prospects and asking the best questions. If you follow a couple of simple guidelines you should have no trouble picking a joint venture partner that will truly have your company's success at heart, together with his/her own.

The first thing you'll wish to try to find in a prospective joint venture partner is credibility. In order for you to reap any benefit from a joint venture you need to team up with somebody who has a strong, recognized relationship with their customers. This must include a record of exceptional customer service before, during and after their sales.

When you've established a requirement for what kind of organisation individual you'll wish to participate in a joint venture with you can begin looking. You want to discover somebody who's developed in a market that's related to the industry you remain in, nevertheless you do not desire them to be in direct competitors with you. Remember, the purpose of a joint venture is to be able to enhance one another's businesses and this is best achieved by using associated services or products, but not ones that are almost identical.

You want to choose a venture partner whose customer base is significantly large to endorse your services or products. It would be rather pointless to partner with a company that has relatively few customers.

As you can see it's not a complicated process that you need to go through to find a joint venture partner. The most essential consider selecting a venture partner is to do your research, ask your questions and get your answers prior to partnering with anyone. It would be all too simple to make a spontaneous decision that could take your possibly highly successful company and quickly turn it upside down and creating much more work for you than you would've had going it on your own.

Tips on Getting JV Partners

Joint venture partners are easy to discover. In fact, there are numerous, many people out there who would happily enter into a joint venture partnership. In order to get a partner, you require to know what a potential partner is looking for and where to discover them.

Suggestion one: Be the sort of individual that you would want to partner up with. This covers several various aspects of who you are, however there are 2 that are in the forefront of many people's minds. The first and probably essential aspect is whether you're reliable. People don't want to work with somebody they feel they might not have the ability to trust. Second, people want someone who takes their service seriously. No one wishes to do business with an individual who's not dedicated to making the partnership work.

Suggestion two: Be attractive as a possible partner; you should have a service that has something to offer in a collaboration. Your business should have a good track record, as should you. This covers not only the quality of your services or products, however also the quality of your customer care in the past, during and after your deals.

After all, one of the many benefits of a joint venture collaboration is the credibility you glean from your partner's reputation.

Suggestion 3: Keep your eyes open for possible partners. You 'd be amazed at all the opportunities you have actually missed out on by not continuously being watchful. Not to mention the variety of opportunities that have escaped you in places that you've merely neglected. Some examples of these places are forums, blogs, and members-only groups that are dedicated to Internet marketing and/or joint ventures. Nevertheless, this does not mean that you should head out and join the first forum or group you stumble upon. As with any organisation associated decision, you'll wish to do a little research initially before joining up.

As soon as you know what kind of individual you're looking for in a joint venture and have an orientation regarding where you may discover them, it should not be long before you're writing a joint venture proposition. Just remember that you must do a little research, ask questions and get the answer before making any decisions on whether to partner up with someone. It's just clever service to understand precisely what you're getting into prior to you make your move.

http://successinternetmarketingagency.com

9

MAKING EVEN MORE CASH WITH RESELL RIGHTS

"Include even more effective income streams to your digital Products and find out how you can make 100% profits offering Products you do not need to produce!"

What is Resell Rights?

The world of Resell or Resale Rights may be brand-new to you. If this holds true, don't stress, you're not alone. Many people are simply discovering reselling and are wondering, like you are, just what Resell Rights are. Let me take a couple of minutes to answer that concern for you.

Resell rights and resale rights are one in the very same. From here on out I will use the term resell rights.

Now that we have actually that cleaned up, let's carry on to what resell rights are.

Resell Rights are unique rights, or authorizations, that are approved to you by way of a legal transaction in between you (the planned reseller) and the owner (the individual with legal right of ownership of the product). In this legal deal you acquire, or otherwise license, the rights to resell the item from the owner. By doing so you are approved to the rights to resell the product to others.

Depending upon which types of Resell Rights you obtain the choices you have in reselling the product might differ. Some Resell Rights permit you just to purchase and resell the products to others, however do not allow your customers to resell the product to anyone else. Other kinds of Resell Rights permit you to buy an item, modify it in any way you choose, and then resell it and its Resell Rights, as your own product, to your clients.

As you can see, there's a great deal of flexibility with Resell Rights Because of this versatility there is likewise a lot of money that can potentially be made with making use of Resell Rights The sky is the limit when you integrate the flexibility of Resell Rights and the unlimited reach of the Internet.

Resell Rights, as they pertain to the Internet, are generally used in reference to e-books and other digital products. The use of Resell Rights with these types of items permits for items to easily be acquired and resold through sites and other Internet channels.

Types of Resell Rights

There are various kinds of resell rights. Resell rights differ from the extremely fundamental right to resell a product to another person to the more versatile rights that allow you to modify an item, rename it, or a lot more. All of these different types of rights can be bought or offered. Let's take some time to briefly go over the 6 main types of resell rights.

• **Give Away Rights**
With this type of rights you can offer an item away free of

charge. Normally, however, you might not resell the product or edit/alter it in any way.

- **Royalty Rights**

This kind of resell rights requires you to pay the author or franchisor of the original product a percentage from each sale of the product that you make. This most often applies to physical products such as books like those you would find in bookstores.

- **Resell Rights**

With this kind of rights you can resell a product. This may apply to physical items in addition to digital items. Normally with digital items you resell the item and keep 100% of the earnings.

- **Standard Resell Rights**

This type of resell rights enables you to resell the product. Nevertheless, your customers do not have any rights to resell the item to anyone else. With this type of rights you keep 100% of the profit you make with each sale.

- **Private Label Rights**

This is probably the most versatile and searched for type of resell rights. When you buy Private Label Rights you purchase the right to alter the product in any way you want, normally. Examples of this are: putting your own name or business label on it, offering resell rights to the product to others as your own, using the product as a structure for your own products.

- **Master Resell Rights**

With this kind of resell rights you have the capability to resell the product together with its Basic Resell Rights to your customers. This likewise enables your consumers to resell the product to others, such as their own consumers. What makes Master Resell Rights appealing to many is the fact that the

Master Resell Rights can be sold alone, or in combination with the product itself.

As you can see, resell rights have numerous benefits and supply lots of channels through which you can make money with them. Taking the time to get more information about resell rights could show extremely worthwhile to you.

How to Use Resell Rights in Your Favor

Using Resell Rights as a way of making money is ending up being more and more popular. The key is using Resell Rights in your favor.

The appeal of e-books and other digital items makes the prospect of owning Resell Rights to one or more of them very appealing. Individuals enjoy details, and what much better way to please your existing clients than by providing them with an e-book or other digital item on a subject that you already understand they're interested in.

Too if you're new to Internet marketing you might want to think about Resell Rights as an option. Information items are hot sellers in nearly every specific niche market.

And although it's not a rock solid marketing research approach, looking into the most popular e-books will offer you an excellent feel for the existing need in certain markets. While doing this you can likewise get a great idea of what sort of e- books and other digital items are offered for you to utilize in conjunction with your organisation's products.

Now there are a couple of ways I 'd like to mention that Resell Rights can work in your favor. The very first, and most likely most obvious, is that you can generate income by reselling the product you have rights to, or reselling the item and its rights, depending on which type of rights you've bought. This works rather well for many people, especially when you've purchased a high quality product.

The second way having Resell Rights can work in your favor is by assisting you in developing a reputation for credibility and integrity with your consumers.

Marketing is needed, but it doesn't carry the trustworthiness it as soon as did. On the other hand, if you have information in print that you can provide your customers or prospective clients, you're offering them a level of know-how that can't be found in a standard ad.

There's also a market for a company based entirely on reselling items. The competition in reselling digital items may be excellent, however you can undoubtedly make a name for yourself if the quality of your products surpasses that of your rivals.

What to Try to find in a Resell Rights Product Before Investing

Prior to purchasing a Resell Rights item you'll want to actually do your homework. With so many items readily available for purchase with Resell Rights it's very easy to become overwhelmed and make a bad financial investment. There are a few factors you should take into consideration prior to investing your hard-earned money in a Resell Rights item.

The first thing you'll want to analyze is what type of Resell Rights is offered with the item you're considering. There are numerous various kinds of Resell Rights and you'll need to know prior to you purchase that the item you're purchasing features the type of Resell Rights you're searching for. Read the fine print prior to making your purchase.

Item X might come with limitations on the minimum sales cost that need to be set for it, or the license may forbid you from offering it in mix with other products. Another common restriction disallows a buyer from selling a specific product on auction websites.

Another aspect that can greatly impact your success with Resell Rights products is competition. You'll desire to find out how long the license for the product has been offered and how lots of licenses have actually been sold.

While they may not be the very same precise item, it can greatly detract from the marketability and possible sales of your product. If you discover that there are already a high number of items of this type however you're still determined to buy it, you may desire to consider Private Label Rights for the item.

Last you'll want to try to find a product that has a strong potential for back-end sales. Lots of people try to find products that they can make sales with now, without seeking to the future for recurring sales from the same clients. Do your research to learn the capacity for back-end sales on any items you're considering.

It can imply the distinction between a smart investment with long-term income potential and a one-shot profit.

Stream Store (+Dynamic Posts Plugin)

https://bit.ly/2kr95WM

10
GOING VIRAL WITH VIRAL MARKETING

"Discover What Forces People Discuss You and Your Service Or Product Voluntarily-- Even if They Don't Earn Money to Do it!"

Top Viral Marketing Success Stories

Viral marketing is the term used for any marketing technique that motivates an individual to pass along a marketing message that they have actually received to others, thus creating the capacity for development in the message's exposure and effect. It's called "viral" marketing due to the rapid rate at which the message can be spread out. And while the name may not be appealing or welcoming, the usefulness of viral marketing surely is.

When the message contains something that people discover worthy or beneficial of sharing, viral marketing is effective just. Whether it be a coupon, totally free offer or info it must be of a certain level of quality to entice receivers to share it with others. Without that aspect there would be no desire to pass it along.

The history of viral marketing proves its usefulness in the modern-day marketing world. For years organisation was dependent on word-of-mouth marketing as a marketing approach. When you offered someone a high quality product or offered them with a top notch service you might depend on them telling their household, next-door neighbors and pals, consequently increasing the traffic in your service. But like with the viral marketing these days, you must've had something of value to cause individuals to want to pass your service's name along to others.

The statistics on viral marketing prove its worthiness as a marketing tool. You can easily see where viral marketing can be an incredibly useful marketing tool.

Using this marketing technique on the Internet has brought it to many people's attention simply because of the huge variety of individuals who can be affected by this type of marketing in an exceptionally brief period of time. Thus the great interest everybody has actually taken in it. Consider this, what other technique of marketing could be utilized to reach millions of people in the course of a relatively short amount of time with beside no charge at all to the marketer? And all the while your marketing message is being passed around, the reality that someone is recommending it to another individual by passing it along is a no-strings-attached endorsement. You 'd be difficult pressed to top that with any other marketing technique in use today.

With all the talk, and the buzz, about viral marketing, it appears as though the principle itself is so popular that it, too, is a case of viral marketing success. That's a sort of amusing way to take a look at it, but it is true. Viral marketing is such a success in and of itself that the message of it is being spread throughout the world as ever before. But here I won't hang out informing you about the marketing itself, however rather about a number of the top viral marketing success stories in e-commerce.

These examples will offer you a clue as to how it is done, and why it works so well.

Hotmail is a tremendous success thanks to viral marketing. Well, what made Hotmail such a success was firstly that it was a free service, and free is always attractive. This led Hotmail to become one of the most noteworthy online viral marketing success stories.

Yahoo! is another viral marketing success. Yahoo! took a slightly various method. They used totally free email also, but they focused more of their program around a whole online neighborhood where you could do everything from searching and research study, to home entertainment, chat, online forums, all in addition to the free email accounts they offered to their visitors. Yahoo! later on produced a place to shop online, and even online auctions, however the auctions are no longer functional.

WebMD ended up being a success through viral marketing due to the fact that, in it's niche, it provided reliable and accurate information related to medical requirements and conditions, as well as other informative services related to the medical field. This website, similar to the others, ended up being a viral marketing success because of its dependability, innovation, functions, and all the other qualities that made its visitors rave.

These are a few of the leading online viral marketing success stories. They are still in company today, and I would encourage you to visit them to see simply why this is so.

You may find yourself telling a friend about the site, and

that's what viral marketing is. Remember, none of these success stories really intended viral marketing to be their key.

Crucial Element of Viral Marketing Success

Perhaps you have actually already been to their websites by now and seen a few of the great things they need to provide. Others have actually also done extremely well because of viral marketing, and they deserve notice too. Today it would be an excellent concept to have a look at what produces such success in online services. There are several crucial elements to this, and we will review those in this and two following posts. To simplify into parts, the very first will have to do with what is provided by the company, the second will be about quality and stability, and the third and final area will be about development and the future.

What is offered by an online viral marketing success story? Let's take a look at what the success stories mentioned previously.

Email is the best and most effective way to communicate online. To offer such a service totally free will lead millions to gather together at that site. Another service everyone requires is information. Providing an online search engine is the very best way to do that, especially when the online search engine is detailed and trusted. And who does not require medical details? That's where the third example has actually been so successful.

The point is to believe in regards to providing a product everyone needs. Or, if you are looking at niche marketing, this will still work. Just consider whatever you can provide as a business that everybody because specific niche will need or want.

That's the key to how viral marketing works. In this first section, it is really about what is offered and how impressed people can be by that.

They all tell you they need it to, but can't find it either. The price is good, and you buy it from this business. That's how what is offered by a business is a key to viral marketing success.

When you take a look at the key elements of success in viral marketing, there is more to it than simply providing something everybody needs. Sure, you can provide any service or product for sale, or even totally free, to individuals. And, opportunities are that they will at first show excellent interest. Nevertheless, if what you use isn't backed up by quality, and if your business does not run with a clear track record for integrity, individuals will quickly look elsewhere for what they need. And, in the end, you're organisation will be no success story, however rather the latest failure at the top of the out-of-business heap.

You see commercials and other advertisements all the time where some business is talking about the quality of their service, or the quality of some item they're selling. It's a big deal, because people want to know that whatever they buy is worth what they paid for it.

That actually leads into the point about stability. Suppose that automobile you bought was made by a business that has an outstanding guarantee program. When it broke down, you called the company and they immediately took care of the issue for you, supporting their commitment to great client service and satisfaction after the sale. Now it looks a little bit different, doesn't it? You might be upset about what took place, however they made it right, and you have that service to tell others about. It's actually a matter of whether or not a business is willing to support what is says. When the business is of great integrity, even problems with product sold are not so bad as if the business did not guarantee its product.

So you can see how quality and stability keep the track record of a company in great standing. This is one of the most essential elements for a business when its track record spreads by word of mouth. To be a viral marketing success, these qualities are essential.

Now that we've talked about what it takes to be a viral marketing success in terms of what you offer, and in terms of the quality and integrity of your products and your company, there is one final part to consider. Well, it's really a matter of perception, and we'll cover that shortly.

But as far as innovation goes, this is certainly essential to success. What people need to learn about your company's development is first that you have it, and that your company welcomes development for an atmosphere of constant improvement. It's the idea that the consumer comes to your online business and is continuously finding smart brand-new methods to do things. They do not understand how you came up with the concept, however they're so impressed that they have to go inform everyone they know about it.

The key for you to achieve this kind of success with innovation is research. Companies who are innovative often have teams of people researching various different ideas all the time.

The only distinction is that you might be doing the research study yourself or with a partner. The idea, however, is that you should always be working to enhance what you market to the consumer.

When a company offers something everyone needs or wants, and that company has a culture of quality and integrity, and when the company is constantly finding new ways to improve what they market, a sense of trust is built. It's that kind of trust that tells the consumer that this is a company who's going to be around for a while. Think about this: do you really trust a company that you think will be out of business in a few years?

All of these crucial elements of viral marketing success are about the qualities of the business. That should inform you that it has to do with how you do business, and not about how you control viral marketing, that matters. The reality is, a lot of business who succeed because of viral marketing did nothing about the viral marketing at all. Rather they worked on quality and stability, on offering something for which there was huge need, and on development. That's how you control viral marketing: you control your business till it is worthy of viral marketing success.

Kinds Of Viral Marketing Methods

It goes without saying that, in any ability, any profession, any technique, there are different methods to do everything. This is equally true of viral marketing. There are not just various types of viral marketing, but also numerous methods by which viral marketing is transferred. With that in mind, I wish to talk to you about both.

However, for the sake of simpleness, I'm going to take this first post to discuss the types of viral marketing, and the 2nd article will talk about the method for transferring the viral marketing message. When completed, you must have a clear understanding of how viral marketing works and how you can use this tool for your business.

One type of viral marketing motivates readers to pass along the message they've simply read. Possibility are that you've seen this often times, either in the form of a chain-letter, or in a more subtle request that, if you like what you simply check out and understand someone else who could gain from it, please pass it along to them. This is an extremely effective way to get viral marketing going.

A second type offers you some incentive for getting the word out. This type of viral marketing uses either financial benefits, gifts, discount rates, or something else of value to the reader if they will forward the message to others.

A third type of viral marketing is not encouraged, but rather is all about the quality of the experience the consumer had. This type is simple word of mouth, and it tends to be the most effective.

A last type I wish to discuss is one you won't see the majority of the time. It's everything about getting individuals to find the surprise message in something, whether that thing is a phrase or a picture or whatever else it may be. It's all about getting people talking first. Individuals enjoy a great mystery, and they begin to discuss with each other what that advertisement must indicate. The message is spread virally before the item is exposed. But once it is exposed, everybody already knows about it and the viral marketing was a success.

There are other variations to this theme of viral marketing types. Nevertheless, amongst all the types out there, these are the most typically used, and the most successful, too. As promised, in the next area I will inform you about how the message is spread out.

Now that you understand the kinds of viral marketing, you will need to comprehend just how the message is spread out. Some of it might have concerned you already just from thinking about the types, however there's a little more to it that we can discuss. With that in mind, let's take a look at the approaches by which the viral marketing messages are transferred from one customer to millions.

One of the most common ways you see this kind of message transmitted on the Internet is through e-mail. You probably see it all the time. A single person receives an email and is motivated to send it to everyone else. They do so by picking everybody in their address book and send the message. Picture if a single person sent to 10 people, and those 10 each to ten more, and it continued. The growth is literally rapid.

You happen across one that is very interesting to you, and you read it. This will get the message out to more people.

Someone, wanting to prove their point, sends a message through with a link in it to some site where that point will be backed up by an article. This is a great way for the message to spread, because everyone in the chat room who's paying attention will probably click that link.

The last significant technique of transmission is actually the most apparent, the most tried and true, and the only one I've mentioned here that does not in fact require use of the Internet. It is, merely, word of mouth. And it does matter that you can get word of mouth going, due to the fact that not everybody is on the Internet routinely.

However, everyone interacts verbally.

So, whatever someone sees on the Internet spreads out not just further in the virtual world, but by word of mouth that message spreads out throughout the real world. It's the oldest, and still the very best, method to get your message spread virally.

Viral Autobots (Bumblebee Edition)

https://bit.ly/2jY3pmX

11
PUBLISHING YOUR OWN MAILING LIST & NEWSLETTER

"With the Internet, It's Possible to Build Your Own Personal Cash Cow from Scratch without Even Joining the Gold Rush!"

Mailing List - Your Personal Gold Mine

A mailing list can actually mean the distinction between success and failure for your online service. Though much of us may be a little unclear by the concept of asking our possible customers for their e-mail address for worry of frightening them off, it's basically a must if you want to get the sort of traffic and make the kind of sales that the truly effective sites have.

You may be wondering why a mailing list is so important, much to mention how it can be a gold mine. Many people don't realize how effective a tool a mailing list has the prospective to be.

Research studies have proven that the common Internet

customer makes around 7 visits to the very same website before lastly making a purchase. When they visit your website, if you get them to opt-in to your mailing list you can stay in touch with them through e-mails and maybe newsletters whereby enticing them back to your website rather than them visiting your competitors.

It does not stop with just luring them back to your website after their initial check out. Another statistic that shows how subscriber list are useful, and can potentially be your individual cash cow is this: roughly 70% of US-based e-mail users have actually bought online after receiving an opt-in based e- mail marketing message.

When you consider how numerous sales you may be missing out on out on right now by not having your own mailing list, that's a pretty powerful fact.

You may be worried about sending out the incorrect message when asking for a customer's e-mail address the statistics speak for themselves. Remember, the people on your mailing list have asked you to send them e-mail, whether they are newsletters, promotions, special offers or updates.

Publishing Your Own Newsletter

Publishing your own newsletter has actually probably crossed your mind on lots of events. The majority of us have actually considered it, and yet numerous still have actually refrained from doing it. There might be a number of various reasons that, but there are much more reasons why you should.

First, let me resolve any misgivings you may have about publishing your own newsletter. It's not nearly as hard an endeavor as you may think. You don't need to send it out weekly, or even every number of weeks. You can have a very successful regular monthly newsletter that the recipients will be pleased with. You also do not need a degree in journalism or English to put out an effective newsletter. While excellent grammar, spelling and punctuation are necessary in effectively communicating with your clients, it's what you're using them on the whole that actually counts. Quality information and deals are what they're actually trying to find.

There's no denying that a newsletter to your customers will entice them to visit your site more often. A free newsletter will make them feel that you truly value them as customers and are rewarding their loyalty.

Your newsletter will not only benefit you by keeping your current customers happy, but if published in the right manner can also send new customers your way. You offer a freebie for discount for new customers in your newsletter and send it to your current, happy and loyal customers.

Along with the factors I have actually already listed, releasing a newsletter also provides a level of competence to you. Your clients will view you as someone who really understands the product and services that you're offering and will assist build a trusting relationship in between you and them. That can benefit you significantly in taking on other more recognized organisations.

As you can now see, publishing a newsletter has many benefits as an online marketing tool. And the effort you present in releasing your newsletter will repay you with substantially higher traffic and sales.

Auto Responders - Your Main Asset

Have you found that you invest more time trying to respond to your clients' emails than you spend on any of your other business jobs? Are your customers getting disappointed with the slow responses to their general emails? If you've addressed "yes" to either of these concerns then you'll understand how automobile responders can be your primary possession.

Auto responders differ from software that runs with your e- mail program to specialized program that is gone through your webhosting's server. Either auto responder will work for a wide variety of standard e-mail tasks. However, if you have unique e-mail requirements that must be satisfied or have a very high volume of email that has to be handled, you may want to consider the auto responder program that's run through your web host.

Say you have a newsletter that your customers can subscribe to. The same can be done with many general information requests, such as requests for price lists, products lists or lists of available services.

Not only do auto responders make quick work of numerous standard e-mail tasks and subscription actions, however they can also be very beneficial in sending batches of other info to your clients. For example, say you've updated your price list and you desire your clients to be familiar with it, or you have actually composed a short article that you wish to go out to all your consumers. You can utilize an auto responder to manage this job for you.

When utilizing an auto responder you can add your own personal signature to the emails that your customers or visitors will get. You can include your name, your company's name, all of your contact information and even a brief message. This works well as a suggestion for your customers. Not to mention, individuals like the personal feel that the signature line adds to your e-mails.

Because they save time and money, auto responders are

your main asset. Not just in the sense that lots of auto responders are totally free, however in the method they make quick, easy work of tasks that could need many hours and several people to accomplish. Just think about all the other work you can be getting done while your auto responder deals with the regular e-mail work for you.

They are likewise a primary property because they avoid your customers from ending up being dissatisfied with the slow action that they would get must you have to manage your e- mails one at a time. And we all know that dissatisfied customers don't visit often, which implies less sales.

How to Release an Effective Newsletter

When it pertains to releasing an effective newsletter there's one primary aspect you require to remember: quality is more vital than amount or frequency. Let me take a minute to discuss this in a little more information.

Despite the fact that your newsletter's primary function may be to drive traffic to your site, you can't disregard the truth that your consumers desire quality. You also require to bear in mind that your newsletter will be an example of your website and business. For that reason quality is a must otherwise you'll simply be lowering your image.

When you begin preparing to publish your newsletter you should consider the content that will be consisted of. You need to use your audience what they want. Put in the time to learn what your subscribers want, require and are interested in obtaining from you. This can be done in a couple of methods.

Ask your visitors what they 'd want most in a newsletter from you. This will not only provide you with the information you need to start your newsletter, but it will also make your customers feel valued.

Second you can e-mail your customers and request for their input. The information you receive from them can be managed in the same manner that you would handle it from the poll or opinion box. This approach will also leave your consumers feeling valued.

Be sure to get your customers to subscribe to your newsletter. Unwelcome e-mail is a sure way to lose customers.

When writing your newsletter, make sure to consist of useful short articles that will interest your subscribers. However, don't exaggerate the articles and neglect essential updates on your site, special offers, or giveaways. Remember, your newsletter will only work for you if it includes something that will constantly bring your subscribers back to your site.

You'll also wish to consist of a little something in each newsletter that can be utilized to attract brand-new visitors. Free offers are always excellent for this. But make sure that you make the offer visible sufficient and luring enough to make your existing subscribers wish to pass it along.

By now you probably have sufficient information to get started on your own newsletter. A great deal of what your newsletter consists of will depend on your consumers desires and requires and your individual choice. Another word of advice, if you haven't gotten an auto responder yet, now might be the time. It will make managing your newsletter much, much easier.

Earning money from Your Mailing List

There are numerous, numerous ways to make money from

your mailing list. Simply having a substantial mailing list is no warranty you'll make money from it, however. The key to generating income from your mailing list to is use it as a tool to not just drive traffic to your site but to lure individuals to make purchases when they go to.

I have a number of tips you can follow to make the most of your mailing list.

The very first component of generating income from your mailing list is to continuously include new names to your list. In order to do this you should have great traffic coming to your website. , if you have a newsletter or regular mailings going out to your customers you can entice them to pass the message along by offering specials or freebies for new subscribers.. You likewise require to ensure that your visitors can easily discover where to register for your mailing list on your website.

The best, most reliable method of making money from your mailing list is with compelling offers. These can be free e-books, newsletters, free articles on a subject related to your products or services or a series of free how-to reports.

When using these free products, be sure to make it understood to the recipient that you encourage and appreciate them passing the message along to others. Be sure to consist of an easy-to-read signature on the e-mail that includes your name, your business's name and all your contact information. As long as the message is high quality and uses something of value your receivers will enjoy to pass it along to others.

There are a couple other methods of earning money from your mailing list that you might wish to consider. Lots of people with large, established subscriber list have relied on leasing, selling and on some events swapping newsletter. A couple of words of warning about using these methods:

1 - Be sure to investigate any laws, regulations or rules governing the exchange of subscriber list.

2-- Consider the emotions of your consumers before using your mailing list for swap, sale or rent. They might feel that their privacy has actually been violated in some manner or another if you do not first get their permission to exchange their info.

As you can see the ways to generate income from your mailing list are neither complex nor extremely time-consuming.

The profits you will reap from an ever-growing mailing list of pleased, devoted customers will undoubtedly be a sufficient benefit for your efforts.

How to Collect Subscribers

If you're looking to develop your online company, one of the most essential tasks you can perform is the task of collecting subscriber leads. Nevertheless, to prevent this from ending up being an overwhelming job, I would advise that you utilize method of collection that put you on auto-pilot. Instead of hand gathering, which can be done, the following methods to gather subscriber leads need setup, and then little extra work for you.

Initially, whenever you established your site, ensure that everyone who visits, whether they come across your website from a search, or if they come through by way of a click-ad, register for either a newsletter or some other kind of periodical e-mailing. Obviously you can not require them to do this, however make sure you totally motivate them to receive all the benefits your website has to offer. In return, you will be getting all the benefits that come from having those critical subscriber leads.

Another method for you to collect subscriber leads is through surveys. Location advertisements about studies on other's sites. When the interested celebration clicks, tell them all about the survey and how they can benefit from it. Then ensure they can only take part if they sign up. This is an appealing method to develop leads, and most people are willing to supply at least an e-mail address for the sake of getting to take a study.

Another way to collect leads is through connecting. You stand to benefit from all of the leads that an affiliate will generate and pass along to you when you participate in an affiliate program.

You will need an opt-in program and an auto-responder when it comes right down to the collection process. These two elements will permit you to collect the info you need and right away send a confirmation email to the brand-new subscriber.

Some people will be apprehensive about providing a name, or a physical address, or a phone number. If you can collect enough information from the subscriber to have at least one way to contact them, you're better off than if you lose them by requiring too much information.

There is another way for you to collect subscriber leads, but be aware that it is not always an efficient one. It's called a mailing list, or a subscriber list, and you can acquire these. Nevertheless, I caution you on these since you may discover that numerous subscribers did not desire their details sold, and you could really damage your reputation on first contact because of this.

It can be effective, but weigh the costs on your own and understand whether it is suitable and allowable for you to get leads in this way.

12

FREE & LOW COST MARKETING METHODS

"Market Your Business on the Internet for MAXIMUM Coverage at MINIMUM Cost!"

Free & Low Cost Marketing - Do They Still Work?

In the world of Online marketing, advertising is crucial to the success of your organisation. And, especially if you're a brand-new start-up looking to get your foot in the door, you require to find the most budget-friendly method to market your business.

Throughout the history of Internet Marketing there have always been affordable and complimentary alternatives to the significant types of advertisement that would require big bucks just to start.

Nevertheless, it might seem these days as if that treasure of free and low-priced marketing is disappearing. But I'm here to guarantee you that it isn't gone. While many types of advertising are ending up being more costly, there are still free and inexpensive techniques that work effectively.

One of the most incredibly reliable methods for advertising, and it is free, is word-of-mouth marketing. Well, some individuals will talk about your business on their own. All you have to do is ask them to inform their friends about your business.

Another low-priced chance for you is affiliate marketing. There will constantly be brand-new affiliates out there aiming to enhance their income and improve their own website. So, you register as an advertiser with an affiliate and your on your method. The factor this is low-priced is due to the fact that you can ultimately decide who promotes for you, and you can pick cost effective strategies that work for you. These affiliates just make money for efficiency, so you only pay when you make money from the advertisement. This holds true of most affiliate marketing.

A third method to use low-cost and complimentary marketing for your company is e-mail marketing. You will only require an opt-in list of interested visitors to your service. What you do from there is simple. You establish emails that include targeted advertisements for your company. You are targeting the most interested customers directly with and advertisement that is well-suited to their interests. The cost of e-mail marketing is so small that it would be absurd not to utilize this method.

Other alternatives exist as well, but not all of them work for every company. The three I have discussed will provide you an excellent starting point (affiliate marketing and viral marketing have actually been gone over in the earlier chapters of this book).

You may wish to search for other means of marketing as well. It's as simple as all the other research you've done to get your business this far if you do. Just keep in mind, some of these other methods are just budget-friendly to some businesses. It all depends upon your business and your objectives.

Writing & Submitting Unique Articles

Composing and submitting articles to the Internet to promote your online service is among the most effective and time- checked means of advertising. The other great feature of articles is that they are often a low-cost, if not totally free way to go. And, whereas other approaches of ad deal little more than the sales-pitch, writing and submitting posts provides the target audience with either information or home entertainment, or possibly both. There are specific things you will want to know about how to write and send short articles effectively.

The first thing you should remember is to keep the short articles short. No standard article should be more than about 500 words, or your audience will lose interest due to the length. Also, keep in mind that a few of the people in your target market might currently have understanding on the subject of your short article, so make sure to research thoroughly and consist of in your writing just the most informative and accurate info.

You want to sound like an expert in your field if you're going to write and submit articles on the Internet to advertise your business. This develops a sense of trust and constructs your track record with customers. That being stated, you ought to make sure, prior to submission, that your short articles are appropriately formatted. Be sure to spell checker and reread the articles to make certain you didn't leave any important information out. Ensure a link back to your site is consisted of someplace in every article. If you can't fit it into the text, put the link at the end of the short article.

When you get ready to submit your articles, you have many options. You want the articles to boost the rankings of your site with search engines, so be sure to include good keywords in them. You can also submit your articles to article submission sites, and these are great.

The more articles you write and submit, the better your chances are for building a solid reputation in your market. The better your reputation, the better your chances are for success as an online business.

Using Traffic Exchanges

When you begin an online organisation, you're seeking to increase your income. Perhaps you're even aiming to make this new endeavor a career. You have actually worked out whatever in addition to you can. You have a prepare for your ad campaign, and you understand it's most likely to work well since you put a lot effort and research into it. But there's one thing you might not have thought about at this point, and it is critical. You will get nowhere in your service without traffic. That's right. Traffic is what Internet service are truly all about. Without traffic, no one will see your website, or what you are offering there. So you need to discover ways to instantly begin bringing in not just traffic, however targeted traffic, to your online company. When you'll realize that you need to join a traffic exchange, this is.

These banners are grouped with the banners of other sites, and you surf to generate traffic to those sites, earning credits for your own site in the process. When others surf and run across your site, they earn credits for generating traffic to your site.

What is important is that you search for the traffic exchanges who have proven their ability to generate traffic that will actually be interested in what your site offers. It is important, on that note, that you choose a site that has a proven track record of bringing real human beings to your site, not just some other computer.

Start with a free membership to one of these traffic exchanges, see how it works, and if you like it, get a paid membership to enhance your success even further. They generate the traffic you need, and you reap the profits. What better way can you think of to have as many as thousands of visitors coming to your site within the first month you're open?

Link Exchanges

Link exchanges are various from other kinds of marketing you have actually done up to this point. Whether you're just getting into your first online organisation, of if you've been doing this for a long time, if you have not gotten into link exchanges, you might be missing out on a great marketing enhancement. These exchanges are something of a cross in between traffic exchanges and affiliate marketing programs. Nevertheless, the method you enter into them and how they work are a bit different.

To begin with, a link exchange offers you the chance to share your links with other sites, and in trade you position their links on your site. There are some brand-new chances emerging that enable you to do this through an exchange website, but most of the time you will have to get in touch with target websites directly and request to the website's webmaster that an exchange be participated in between your site and theirs. With the sites I mentioned, you can avoid most of this e-mail hassle and simply register your site as one ready to enter into a link exchange.

The benefit to being a member of a link exchange is that you are sharing traffic with other sites who are, by your choice, going to give you targeted traffic appropriate to the goals of your service. Furthermore, the more exchange partners you accumulate, the much better exposure you have for your website. And, as you know currently, more presence means more traffic, and more traffic means higher earnings.

You don't want to have a bunch of links out there doing nothing for your business. Getting into link exchanges and maintaining them can be a good thing, but you will have to decide whether the work is worth the reward.

One final note about link exchanges. There are some who have argued that these agreements actually take traffic away from your site by encouraging visitors to click a link before they purchase anything from you. While this may hold true sometimes, it is not the standard. Many webmasters have actually discovered success with link exchanges and would refrain from doing without them. So, here once again, it will depend on you to choose whether this system will be a benefit to your company, and it will depend on you also to decide whether it's working as soon as you've entered it.

Participating in Online forums

Forums are a very popular type of interaction on the Internet. Lots of websites offer topic-specific forums on almost anything you can think of. These are more official places for people to communicate than chat rooms are, so a higher degree of rules applies when you take part in the forum. But they do use you a special opportunity to develop and build your credibility on the subject matter of your option. And, with that, comes the chance to promote your online company in a way just a reliable person can.

Forums are easy to get included with. For the most part it is a simple matter of signing up to get a username and password for the forum. Most often these forums are a complimentary service provided by the hosting site. You can normally publish as typically as you like, and you can check out all of the archived posts made by others. The forum posts are arranged into threads.

What you wish to do to establish a good reputation on the online forum is make informative and logical posts in action to others. If you need to, research the subject prior to you make your post. Bear in mind that this is about your credibility, so you require to make certain that your posts are helpful, precise, and remedied for spelling and grammar. Also, don't scream (all caps). A lot of forum participants dislike yelling.

To effectively use a forum to market your online business, you may wish to include a link in the signature of your posts. This is an automatic way for you to ensure that every post you make has that link in it. If you do, you will find that people who have come to respect and trust what you say will suddenly start complimenting you on your site.

I would strongly advise you not to come into a forum as a new member and instantly start running over the ideas of others. Another no- no is to make your first, or even one of your first, posts a blatant attempt to advertise your site. Forums are one of those opportunities to not only market your online business, but to have some fun and learn new things at the same time.

E-zine Advertising

That fact makes e-zines a terrific place for you to look if you're interested in advertising to generate highly-targeted traffic to your own online business. And the good thing is that there are several ways for you to get involved.

One way for you to get included is through affiliate

marketing. Just as with many other ways of advertising, signing up with an affiliate program puts you in touch with thousands of other businesses online, all of whom are looking either to promote, or to earn money as an affiliate. E-zines are among those who are seeming an affiliate. Just be careful about this: a brand new e-zine will not have nearly as numerous subscribers as an established one, so you may not constantly be getting as much traffic right now as you think.

You can also go around the process of getting into an affiliate program. Go to the sites and take a look at what the e-zine has to offer its subscribers. This will be a key factor in knowing whether this is a good place to advertise if you're looking for high traffic.

Stay away from those who would break your budget plan.

A final way for you to consider entering e-zine advertising is to do all of it yourself. If you have a website where you offer merchandise, think about establishing an e-zine around the products you offer, and the way of life that your clients live. This is a guaranteed way to get targeted traffic as your readership broadens. Just know the quantity of work it will take for you to create and manage an e-zine. Go for it if you feel it's worth the effort. The rewards can often be terrific with these diy ventures.

Press Releases

Among all of the ways to get instant and free publicity for your project, site, or product, press releases have to be one of the most effective methods. This method of advertising, and it really is an advertisement, gets your message out to the entire subscribed readership of whatever publisher decides to print your press release.

Initially, and foremost, you must write the press release. It needs to be well-written and include the who, what, when, where, why, and how of your sale, opening, or whatever else you 'd be announcing. The writing needs to be clear and to the point, efficiently using correct grammar. All words must be checked for spelling. The last thing you desire is to put out substandard work that won't make it past the desk of it's recipient. The publisher has total option in whether or not to publish your press release, so you're going to need to sell him or her on it. Consider having someone else write it for you if you don't feel that you have the ability to write an effective press release. Sure, you may have to pay a cost for the service, but the benefits of a good press release make it well worth whatever you may need to pay.

As soon as you have the press release written, you will need to know where to send it. To do this you will need to put together the contact info of all the publishers you will desire the release to go to. The most effective method for you to do this is with an online search. A lot of everybody these days has a website for their service, and publishers of news and other composing are no exception. So get that list together, and send the release to each of them in the format they need. Remember that you may need to change the file several times to satisfy the requirements of individual publishers.

You might be called about the press release. Answer their questions politely and thoroughly if you are. They might be searching for a little bit more than what you put in the release, so it is to your advantage to be offered for their concerns. Once they have whatever they need, they will release your press release and potentially countless readers all over the world will understand about what your business is doing. What much better, more immediate method can you think of to do all that?

Using Pay-Per-Click (PPC).

Or, you may have been reading an e-mail or an article and you noticed a hyperlink included in the text. If you clicked on that banner or hyperlink and went to another site, you probably just made the site owner some money. Let's take a look at how you can use PPC to advertise your business.

PPC advertising is one of those great, low-cost ways for you to market either your products, or your entire site to people on the Internet. You then provide this banner to the sites who are willing to advertise for you. When traffic comes to their site, and notices the banner, they are likely to click on it.

These are the programs where all manner of Internet business go to either be or advertise and affiliate for advertisers. You want to have the most traffic you can, and you want that traffic to be targeted.

The best way to know whether you are in a reputable program is to look online and especially in forums for clues as to the integrity of the program and its participants. As I said, it's not going on everywhere, so just use caution, and you'll find yourself receiving much targeted traffic for a very low price.

13
IN CLOSING

"Going Online and Taking Your Share of the E-Commerce Pie!"

Summary

As this book draws to a close, I rely on that you now understand much better the idea of marketing online.

Incredibly, in a number of ways, marketing online reflects a lot of similarities in marketing offline. Perhaps, the most significant distinction is the idea of taking your marketing knowledge online where the Web connects every one from all over the world, offering us bigger and many more opportunities.

To get you started online quickly, I've committed the last pages of this book to awesome Web Service resources I proudly suggest to you. I hope you will find them helpful as they have been for me.

Having stated that, I wish you all the very best in your brand-new adventures and endeavors.

To Your Online Marketing Success!

http://successinternetmarketingagency.com

You can reach us by:

Email: successinternetmarketingteam@gmail.com
Phone: 302-504-4257

ABOUT THE AUTHOR

In my professional experience, I had the opportunity to set up & manage a team of online marketers catering to all kinds of online marketing needs in the industry. I really enjoy working with entrepreneurs and business owners because of the challenges they pose and the way we plan and execute with the limited resources to contribute to their growth.

This book is intended to assist Entrepreneurs/Business Owners in getting an insight into the importance of Online Marketing in any Economies and how to go about it. The Internet Marketing Manifesto - Everything you wanted or needed to know about internet marketing on the world's #1 platform is a comprehensive collation of data of different marketing options available and the kind of support extended by us at different levels. It also provides an insight into the importance of Online presence, Social Presence, SEO, SEM, Facebook Business Page, Facebook Campaigns for Lead Generation, etc.

You can also get an insight into the kind of Support & Services we provide and the need for Business Coaching, Business Consulting, Mentoring Advisory & Implementation Support for facilitating the growth in businesses and entrepreneurs. With Success Internet Marketing Agency and the team... www.successinternetmarktingagency.com.

Made in United States
Orlando, FL
04 November 2026

90203666R00083